D0676924

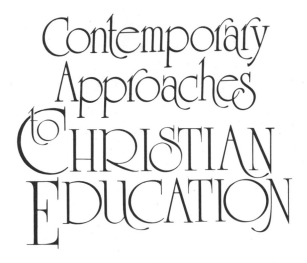

Contemporary Approaches to CHRISTIAN EDUCATION

Jack L. Seymour
and
Donald E. Miller
with

Sara P. Little
Charles R. Foster
Allen J. Moore
Carol A. Wehrheim

Abingdon Press
Nashville

CONTEMPORARY APPROACHES TO CHRISTIAN EDUCATION

Copyright © 1982 by Abingdon

98 99 00 01 02 03—15 14

This book is printed on recycled acid-free paper.

Library of Congress Cataloging-in-Publication Data

SEYMOUR, JACK L. (JACK, LEE), 1948-
    Contemporary approaches to Christian education.
    Includes bibliographical references.
    1. Christian education—Philosophy—History—
20th century—Addresses, essays, lectures.
    I. Miller, Donald Eugene. II. Title.
    BV1464.S48   207   81-14899   AACR2

ISBN 0-687-09493-3 (pbk.)

The chart on pages 32 and 33 and portions of chapter 1 are revised versions of material which appeared in the Spring 1979 issue of *The Chicago Theological Seminary Register*. Used by permission.

Scripture quotations are from The New English Bible, © the Delegates of the Oxford University Press and the Syndics of the Cambridge University Press 1961, 1970. Reprinted by permission.

MANUFACTURED IN THE UNITED STATES OF AMERICA

Acknowledgments

Earlier versions of the chapters of this book were presented as papers at a consultation on the future of Christian education held in Chicago in the fall of 1980. We wish to express appreciation to the agencies that sponsored the consultation: Bethany Theological Seminary, Chicago Theological Seminary, Garrett-Evangelical Theological Seminary, McCormick Theological Seminary, Northern Baptist Theological Seminary, Chicago Baptist Association of the American Baptist Church, Church of the Brethren, Episcopal Diocese of Chicago, Northern Illinois Conference of The United Methodist Church, Presbytery of Chicago of the United Presbyterian Church in the U.S.A., and Chicago Metropolitan Association of the United Church of Christ. Particular thanks go to Charlotte Alderson and Virginia Less, who saw that the conference ran smoothly.

As a result of the dialogue at the conference, this book is a genuinely cooperative enterprise. The suggestions from our contributors, as well as others shared during discussions, inspired many of the conclusions in the last chapter.

Contents

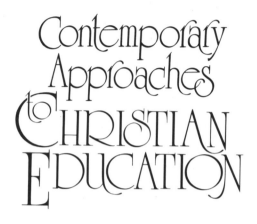

1

Approaches to Christian Education
Jack L. Seymour

Described in this introductory chapter are five ways contemporary Christian educators approach the theory and practice of Christian education: religious instruction, faith community, development, liberation, and interpretation. While these approaches are not exclusive of one another and do not represent all the ways Christian education can be defined, they do illustrate primary metaphors used to understand the task of Christian education. The thesis of this volume is represented in this first chapter—that a better understanding of the perspectives by which Christian education is being organized will contribute to shaping a more comprehensive and coherent theory and practice of Christian education. The hope is that this volume will stimulate dialogue among Christian educators as to the future shape of the discipline.

The last decade has seen considerable development in Christian education. A new sense of hope has replaced the despair of the early 1970s and is evidenced by contemporary attention to the search for future options for Christian education theory and practice.

Examples of this hopefulness are plentiful. There is an increase in scholarly research in Christian education, exhibited by the establishment of Religious Education Press, a publisher exclusively for religious education material; and the founding of *Annual Review of Research: Religious Education,* a journal to report the findings of empirical research in religious education. In addition, significant disciplined reflection upon alternative approaches to Christian education is taking place. For example, one task force of professors is struggling with the question of the nature of the academic discipline of Christian education. Other authorities are examining alternative concepts of the relationship of Christian education to public education, to Christian theology, to religious studies, and to the institutional church.[1] Concurrently, thought is being given to approaches that might improve the quality of Christian learning and living. While considerable research has centered on enhancing the traditional schooling approaches to church education, there also have been new approaches proposed which emphasize such diverse concerns as defining how the faith community is the locus of Christian education, how spiritual development is an agenda for Christian education, how Christian education inspires the quest for political and social justice, and how the Christian tradition can be made meaningful in the present cultural and social context.

These developments are in direct contrast to the mood with which Christian education entered the 1970s, as expressed in an article by Iris Cully, a respected Presbyterian educator. Entitled "What Killed Religious Education," that article described the "passing" of religious education, as illustrated by the decrease of seminary and denominational positions in education, a lessening of ecumenical cooperation, and a decline in publishing for religious education.[2] Many felt that the discipline faced such a serious crisis that a search for a new identity for the field was initiated. At present, the fruits of that search are being seen. By no means has an identity been established, but effort is being expended in the cause. The following set of articles is intended to clarify some of the new directions proposed for the field and to offer guidance for the continuing quest.

Approaches to Theology and Education

In the human sciences, considerable attention has been given to the way persons come to experience and define reality. A conviction emerging from this research is that human beings construct models, paradigms, and myths which serve as interpretive frameworks to help them limit, organize, and act upon impressions.[3] In short, these models, constructed from personal life stories and understandings of reality taught by the culture, provide lenses through which the world is focused, and define patterns, experiences, and facts to which individuals must respond.

On the basis of this research, it has become clear that the uncovering and analysis of interpretive frameworks are of utmost importance because these frameworks and the metaphors they employ define the way reality is structured. For example, in empirical research, the veracity or usefulness of the "facts" discovered and the conclusions reached are directly limited by the interpretive framework, theories, and method employed in the research process itself. These frameworks and their metaphors constitute reality.

One way to define the identity of an academic discipline is to explore the frameworks and metaphors used by its practitioners. Such studies have been initiated in several fields, including theology and education. David Tracy's *Blessed Rage for Order* and James MacDonald's "Transcendental Developmental Ideology of Education" are two examples of this method of analysis.[4]

Tracy surveys models of theology in order to understand the increasing pluralism, as well as to provide a way to redefine the theological task. He describes four recent historic options, which he labels orthodox theology, liberal theology, neo-orthodox theology, and radical theology, and then proposes a revisionist model. He examines how these theologies understand the nature of the Christian tradition and how they relate to contemporary understandings of human existence. Through his descriptions, Tracy hopes to illumine their strengths and weaknesses in addressing theology's contemporary problems, thus providing a way to understand the shape of theology as well as the issues that need continuing reflection. He feels that the revisionist position he proposes will critically correlate Christian tradition and human experience, thereby addressing the central problem of modern theological construction—that of exploring "the dramatic confrontation, the mutual illumination and corrections, the possible basic reconciliation between the principal values, cognitive claims, and existential faiths of both a reinterpreted post-modern consciousness and a reinterpreted Christianity."[5]

James Macdonald has offered education a similar exploration. He argues that the primary problem for educators has been the defining of the relationship between the person and the culture, or in other words, between inner experience and outer experience. The attempt to resolve this problem has launched alternate models by which to understand education. He lists five approaches to education: romantic, cultural transmission, developmental, praxis, and transcendental developmental. In actual practice, teaching style and decisions about educational curricula are influenced by one's predominant model.

The romantic and cultural transmission models are defined as naïve views. The romantic is concerned with the unfolding of the individual's capacities: It places all attention on inner experience, and its educational model emphasizes granting maximum freedom to the individual to develop innate capacities. The cultural transmissive, its direct opposite, is grounded exclusively in the world of external experience; education is the process of injecting cultural values into the learner.

In contrast, the developmental and praxis models note the inextricable relationship of inner and outer experience, but still tend to see the predominant emphasis in the relationship from one perspective or the other. The developmental ideology highlights the person's internal structures which are called into development by external experience. Thus education initiates a process by which these inner capacities are called into being, tested, and expanded. On the other hand, the praxis model emphasizes that the structures of social life define the processes of development, learning, and life-chances. Based on a social critique of education, the model suggests approaches to educational praxis which enhance the learner's awareness of cultural and value transmission. While both the developmental and praxis models are in conversation with each other, one emphasizes biological structures while the other looks primarily at structures of social life.

Macdonald proposes a fifth model (a revisionist one, to use Tracy's phrase) called a transcendental developmental ideology. It is a hermeneutical model with inner experience and outer experience equally emphasized. Macdonald feels that neither exists independently of the other. While one's external experience consists of the facticity of the world, what is experienced is limited by an internal lens that defines which sensations will be experienced and which will not. On the other hand, while one's internal experience is made up of biological growth and personal history, it is also framed by the social reality within which one is formed. Therefore, the aim of education defined by this model is "a centering of the person in the world . . . or the creation of meaning that utilizes all the potential given to each person."[6] Education then must spend more time helping persons understand, explore, and enhance the patterns by which they organize their meaning. Macdonald's approach to education is an extension of the research on modeling itself. Education helps persons explore and analyze the way they create models to function within the biological and social world of human existence. It focuses on the transaction of inner and outer experience.

Both Tracy and Macdonald offer ways to understand their disciplines and to shape further research. Such a comparable analysis of Christian education could also be helpful in understanding how it has understood itself, how it has defined the word *education*, and how it has approached the tasks of educating, forming, or initiating persons into Christian faith and life.

Approaches to Christian Education

Several variables could be considered in organizing an exploration of Christian education. One could look at the way theology is defined, the way the Bible is used, or the way such education is engaged. In this particular study, we will examine the key metaphors that have been used to define the aim and purpose of Christian education throughout its history. Secondarily, we will explore questions about the role of the teacher, the nature of the learner, and the context within which Christian education takes place.

Five approaches will be surveyed: religious instruction, faith community, spiritual development, liberation, and interpretation.[7] While these approaches are not fully parallel and certainly are not mutually exclusive, they do illustrate that different emphases suggest differing strategies for Christian education, and more important, they focus on different questions as critically significant in shaping the discipline and its practice. Simply stated, each approach uses a different metaphor. Respectively, they are education, community of faith, person, justice, and meaning. The characteristics of each approach will be examined and will be illustrated by a contemporary representative.[8] The predominant contribution and issue raised by each approach will be suggested.

Religious Instruction

The primary metaphors used in the religious instruction approach are drawn from the discipline of education. The proponents of this approach usually emphasize that the teaching/learning transaction consists of the transmission of Christian religious beliefs, practices, feelings, knowledge, and effects to the learner, and the context is the church's educational programs.

The discipline of education is thought to provide the structure for a comprehensive program of Christian education. The assertion of James Michael Lee, a Catholic educator, is illustrative: "Religion teaching is basically no different from any other kind of teaching. Nor is the learning of religion basically different from any other kind of learning."[9]

In fact, since the middle of the nineteenth century when the Sunday school was first defined as the church's agency for Christian education, to be concerned with the evangelization and nurture of children and adults, the educational quality of the church's instructional program has been in question. In the 1860s, J. M. Gregory reflected this agenda for the church educational program:

> The Sunday School is not an isolated and eccentric movement of human benevolence. . . . It is but a part—the religious part—of that great movement of the age which has organized the common school systems of the world, and is everywhere marshaling the forces of civilized peoples and governments for the education of the rising generations. And as the common, public schools are steadily mounting an ever advancing wave of popular regard, to greater efficiency and strength, to better methods and nobler works; so must the Sunday School, born of the great fundamental ideas and borne onward by the same growing power of popular opinion, advance to new and riper forms of work and to a new and richer fruitage.[10]

A parallel relationship was defined between the public school and the church's school, which still continues to inform understandings of Christian education.

Today public education is the primary image which occurs to many people when the subject of Christian education is discussed. A church, for example, feels fortunate when it can recruit schoolteachers for its program, because they are expected to be already trained in the best approaches of education to use in the church's program. While the tasks of public and church education are distinguished by the fact that one is secular and the other religious, the findings of educational research are seen as being of primary importance for church education practice, and many church schools are judged on assumptions drawn from public education. Volunteer and untrained teachers, as well as inadequate curricula and lack of educational supervision, are identified as major problems.

One illustration of the religious instruction approach is the complex and sophisticated Christian education theory of James Michael Lee. Lee recognizes the roles that Christian tradition, the life of the church, and the experiences of transcendence play in any educational ministry of the church; yet he argues that religious instruction is a subdiscipline of social science, rather than of theology. For Lee, religious instruction is a comprehensive term, denoting that the church educator should draw on insights from developmental, sociological, and educational research, as well as from theology. Religious instruction is the process by which a student's behavior is modified so that he or she can "acquire behaviors which we may legitimately term 'Christian.' "[11] The goal is the religious growth of a person into full participation in the Christian life. The process by which a student's capacities and needs are assessed, and through which experiences are structured to enable growth, is an instructional process. The teacher is the facilitator of specified behavioral goals.

Lee's description of the teaching/learning process is comprehensive. He provides both a thorough description of the way persons learn and an instructional theory to help teachers facilitate religious growth. For him, the theory of teaching and the theory of learning are distinct.[12] Teaching theory is built on knowledge about learning, but it consists of knowledge of the variables and conditions that effect learning, how these can be effectively structured in a situation to bring about the learning of particular variables, and what concrete skills are required by the teacher.

The goals of the theory are also comprehensive. The student's cognitive, affective, conative, and life-style behaviors all are to be influenced. In other words, the teacher is to consider what knowledge and understanding the student has gained, how faith and thought have been integrated, what Christian values and attitudes have been acquired, what level of theological maturity is evidenced, and what patterns or operations of living have been formed.

To effect such behavioral change, the teacher is called to structure the student's learning environment.[13] Lee calls this environment the Christian living laboratory, for here in a formal learning situation, the student experiences Christian living and, under supervision, can test present or possible styles of thinking, feeling, valuing, and living.

A high concern for professionalism pervades Lee's work. He feels that too much past religious education has been conducted unsystematically, by well-meaning people who lacked the skills to effect Christian learning. He demands educational and theological rigor to discover the shape of Christian teaching, and he insists on proficiency in instruction. "The religion teacher in the field not only ought to be adequately grounded in the science of religious instruction but also must possess to a sufficiently high level the proficiency skills involved in facilitating religious behaviors in learners."[14] Lee's theory of religious instruction demonstrates that Christian education can learn and profit from a serious study and application of educational theory and practice.

The primary metaphors of the religious instruction approach are thus drawn from educational theory. The language of education applies as much to this model as it does to public education. Christian educators are reminded of the real importance of educational research for Christian education praxis. Nevertheless, this approach must be very careful with its theory of the relationship between theology and the human sciences, else the power of theology to shape reality may be ignored or transcended by the power of education.

Faith Community

The faith community approach uses very different resources to define the aim of Christian education. The very nature of the Christian community is thought to define the appropriate procedures for *church* education. The unique contours of the faith community itself become the contours of the education program.

Since the church's educational ministry developed its

form in relation to public education, some church leaders have complained that its goals and procedures have been distorted. For example, in 1872, Edward Eggleston, the American Sunday school editor and author, challenged the very idea of a uniform lesson curriculum. He felt that "the spiritual influence of the Sunday-school" would be lost in the "attempt to put on the Sunday-school, the yokes of the day-school classification, and grading, and making the amount of knowledge the test."[15] For him, the aim of the church's school must be primarily spiritual, rather than instructional. This critique of what was felt to be an overreliance on the school and on education has continued to reassert itself throughout the history of American Christian education.

The attitude is reflected in John Westerhoff's criticisms. He claims that a schooling-instructional paradigm has victimized Christian education and imprisoned it in secular pedagogy.[16] His community of faith-enculturation paradigm is meant to be a clear alternative. Westerhoff stands in a grand tradition of Christian educators who look to the faith community as the context, content, and method for Christian education theory and practice. Westerhoff, in fact, does not call the discipline Christian education, substituting instead the word *catechesis* to signal clearly that the discipline is concerned with the way persons are initiated and grow into the Christian faith community.[17]

Of course no one can, nor would anyone want to avoid the use of educational theory; rather, the desire is to put education in its proper perspective. Eggleston himself used common school innovations in his curricula, and Westerhoff draws heavily on the anthropology and sociology of education. Yet Westerhoff feels that to take sociology of education seriously demands significant attention to the theological issues of the nature of the Christian tradition, the form of the Christian community, and the operative symbols and rituals of that community.

For Westerhoff, socialization, or more properly, enculturation, is much more than an educational strategy. It illumines the very nature of the Christian community. It raises questions about the character of the Christian community, the kind of leadership it inspires, and the symbols, myths, and rituals that give it life and mission. This approach to Christian education is shaped by the embodiment of Christian faith in the form of the church. Decisions about initiation and nurture are made on the basis of the structures and patterns of life in the faith community.

As Westerhoff defines catechesis, these differences are highlighted. For him, catechesis is a pastoral activity rather than an educational activity. Its task is to transmit the faith of the church in such a way that it is intentionally and vitally embodied in persons and in their church. He states directly that the language of education and instruction is not helpful, for the process really is one of enculturation, in which a community attempts to aid a person to accept and internalize its values, beliefs, and way of life.[18]

Yet it is just as rigorous a process as is education, and just as intentional, systematic, and sustained, valued and based on the interaction of persons. Its primary question is not of teaching and learning, but, "What is it to be Christian together in community and in the world?"[19] Catechesis is concerned with conversion, with persons owning the Christian faith and seeking to fulfill its demands.

Therefore to effect Christian believing and living in a person, he or she must experience an "intentional, covenanting, tradition-bearing faith community."[20] A person will be immersed in the Christian story, the patterns of living, the rituals and symbols, and the actions and mission of the faith community, to experience how reality is defined and how life is given meaning. Tradition is thus a key word. From the tradition comes the content and process of Christian faith—the Christian stories and the Christian rituals.[21] For the Christian church, these stories and rituals are the means by which the contemporary experience of the life, death, and resurrection of Jesus is re-presented, embodied, and learned.

In the faith community approach, Christian education becomes the natural process through which a community embodies its faith and passes it on from generation to generation. There seems little need to introduce alien educational settings into the faith community, for if the church is living its faith adequately, its perspective on reality will be taught. This approach reminds Christian educators that the very shape of the church is the primary setting and resource for education. It cautions them to respect the natural but intentional processes by which the faith is shared and maintained. The primary questions that this approach should address are: How is a prophetic word heard? How is the community itself transformed? While representatives state that the faith community approach is a dialectic of transmission and transformation, it is difficult for them to state how this process of transformation occurs.

Spiritual Development

While many Christian educators develop their theory in relationship to the content and methods of the institutions thought to carry Christian education—that is, the school or church—others focus instead on the religious experience and religious quest of the individual as being the proper aim of Christian education. The person's spiritual life is the purpose and the context for education.

Again, this theme is found throughout the history of Christian education. Since the time when life-cycle development was taken seriously by Christian educators, the religious quest of the individual has been regarded as a primary task for Christian education. Contemporary concern about this agenda can be seen in the controversy faced by many local churches in deciding between Bible-based and life-centered curricula. These controversies can be traced to the birth of a full-fledged developmental approach in the progressive era at the beginning of the twentieth century. At that time, the individual's life experience was advocated as the orienting principle for Christian teaching, in contrast to the Bible-content approach of the uniform lesson curriculum. The classic curriculum statement of the era took "the experience of

growing persons" as its starting point.[22] While recognizing
the importance of the Bible and the tradition, this new
theory emphasized that the religious experience of the
student was primary. Of course, experience needed to be
guided, enriched, and expanded in the process of education, but it was the experience, as well as the capacities for
growth inherent in the individual, which were to be the
bedrocks upon which education was built. These developmental educators felt that the church should discover and
address the variety of settings within the person's life which
enabled the growth of religious experience; therefore, the
need for individualized guidance was highlighted. Graded
curricula resulted. Yet developmentalists argued that it was
not enough merely to use knowledge of development to
sequence the teaching of external content, but that the
individual's internal experience in the world and with God
were to be the primary content.

The contemporary application of both humanistic methods of education and developmental research to Christian
education are expressions of this position. Gloria Durka and
Joanmarie Smith, both Catholic religious educators, define
the two basic assumptions which undergird a developmental model of education as "the principle of growth and
the successive, sequential expansion of experience on
different levels."[23] They demonstrate that the work of
psychologists such as Erikson, Kohlberg, and Piaget, and of
theologians of human development such as Fowler, are
used to frame an approach to Christian education based on
a commitment to continuing growth.

Several Christian educators—James Fowler, Donald
Miller, James and Evelyn Whitehead, Mary Wilcox—could
illustrate this approach.[24] In the work of each, an effort is
made to apply moral or faith development theory to
Christian learning. The ordered process of development of
a person's experience is seen as the setting within which
Christian education takes place. The content of the faith, the
institutions of Christian learning, and the methods of
expanding, enriching, and reflecting on experience are very
important, but the crucial questions are: How will a person

experience and understand this content, ritual, symbol, or lesson? How will he or she shape it into a personal meaning and faith system? The language Ross Snyder made prominent for Christian education in the 1960s is illustrative here.[25] For example, one is challenged to be faithful to a personal story and vocation, to build out of the persons, traditions, and objects one encounters a "personal life-world" which becomes one's destiny. It is recognized that each person must make a decision about the values, beliefs, and traditions that will define his or her style of life. Here the personal appropriation of meaning and personal definition of a life vocation are emphasized.

This approach is also concerned with the significant personal crises through which persons must pass in acquiring faith and with the ways cultural and religious understandings are integrated into a personal perspective on reality. In the last few years, this approach has benefited significantly from the Catholic spiritual-formation movement. Through this movement, Christian education has acquired methods to enable growth as a spiritual and religious, as well as a human project. It seems that the practice of spiritual direction is becoming a primary metaphor for the teaching/learning transaction.

One of the clearest contemporary examples of this approach in action is *Centerquest*, a curriculum prepared by The Educational Center in St. Louis.[26] Drawing on research in religious development and Jungian psychology, this curriculum uses Bible stories and contemporary literature as tools for stimulating the recall and expression of religious experiencing, and for self-conscious reflection on and development of one's inner resources for religious living. The actual content of the stories and of the Christian tradition are seen as secondary to the internal feelings of the person. The lessons are not viewed as vehicles to teach any specific content, but are to stimulate the person's own internal spiritual growth.

The spiritual development approach reminds Christian educators of the role religious experience plays in Christian learning. Too often, it has been neglected as a resource in shaping educational programs. It also reminds educators of the need to reintegrate spiritual formation into educational theories and programs. Christian educators many times have emphasized contemporary psychological resources over spiritual resources for growth. In some versions, however, the approach can become narcissistic, with private spirituality substituting for social concern; and theologically, the approach must wrestle with the way an individual's experiences are integrated with the wealth of experience present in the church's tradition.

Liberation

Justice is the primary metaphor used by liberation educators. The social context of suffering and exploitation, of dehumanization and oppression, are to set the agenda for the church's educational ministry. Liberation educators begin with the biblical promise and vision of the kingdom of God. This vision, combined with a social analysis, is to inspire the mission of the church.

The goal is to enable the church and its members to be faithful to the calling of the Kingdom and to recognize forms of oppression. It is feared that too often the vision that motivates the church and its members is of the secular world, rather than of the Kingdom. It is felt that persons become lost in the comforts of daily life and the "busy-ness" of church life, thereby forgetting the unjust distribution of resources and the inequality of life-chances. Traditional Christian education is criticized as deficient because it tends to deal with privatistic individualism and with unembodied content, both of which insulate church members from the harsh realities of the world.

This same critique was leveled at Christian education more than one hundred years ago when the Sunday school was transformed from a mission school for the poor and isolated into an educational agency for the church's members. In the 1860s, Henry Ward Beecher, the pastor of Plymouth Church in Brooklyn, pleaded with church leaders not to forget the original mission purpose of the Sunday school. He was convinced that it was the responsibility of the church to seek alleviation of moral hurt and social pain.

> Through mission schools will be reached thousands that will not be reached by the Church alone. . . . [H]ere is the way we Protestants *must* bring the Church to bear on the whole country, and utilize our men and women in such a way that the poor shall have the Gospel preached to them, the unfortunate shall be relieved, and the great moral sores in our cities shall be healed.[27]

Recurrently, the themes of mission and social justice have become primary agendas for Christian education. Neither the individual's needs nor the church's content are to determine the style of education, but the response of the gospel to the social situation. Malcolm Warford of Eden Theological Seminary defines the task of liberation Christian education as "the continuing praxis of evoking the church's growth as a liberating community and encouraging the development of critical consciousness."[28]

Responding to liberation theology and emerging contextual forms of education, this approach recognizes the power of a social situation to define reality, maintain privilege, and limit the alternatives for hope and social transformation. It encourages a style of education that provides persons with the tools of critical consciousness—to see how reality is being defined, to analyze the reasons for this definition, and to be empowered to act for social transformation in line with the prophetic witness of the gospel.

Drawing heavily on the work of the Brazilian educator Paulo Freire, this approach criticizes most forms of education and defines them as "banking" models, since they deposit knowledge, patterns, and values into persons but do not give them the tools to shape their own reality. True education is thought to be liberating because it helps persons shape the reality within which they live. Therefore the methods of education and the style of the teacher must respect the learner from the very beginning and must see education as a collegial and dialogical process of creating reality.

The work of several Christian educators represent this position. In addition to Warford, one can examine the work of Grant Shockley and Brian Wren. The key words used to characterize this view are *context*, *praxis*, and *vision*.[29] The liberation position regards the social construction of reality as very significant, feeling that any knowledge is socially conditioned; therefore, when one educates, one is professing a value, cultural, and political position. Education is not neutral. Social injustice is submerged within the very content taught about a culture; myths of what is inevitable are perpetuated in hidden ways. The task of a liberating education is to pose the political, social, and cultural context as a problem for action and analysis, so that the context can be opened. The primary strategies of education are hermeneutics of suspicion and critical action-reflection with the people in a context. An educator works in concert with the people in the context, to understand how reality is formed and can be transformed.

In the model, Christian education is expanded beyond reflection or instruction to be a praxis—an action and reflection. Concrete involvement for change in the context is combined with analysis and reflection. In this approach, education becomes a proactive discipline which critically and constructively shapes reality.

Finally, liberation education is empowered with a vision. While it does denounce the situation of social injustice, it also announces the new reality that can be built. Jesus' resurrection is seen as an example of the renewing transformation that God is effecting in the world. The vocation of the Christian educator is to be with others in the criticism of the present in light of God's promise of *shalom*. Christian education becomes a prophetic task: the transforming of life toward *shalom* takes precedence over the transmission of content.

Through Christian education, it is hoped that persons will be able to analyze their life commitments and those of the church, to reflect on that which defines the meaning seen in life, and to engage in effective means of transforming social and political structures for justice. The approach clearly recalls the prophetic commitment at the heart of Christian faith—the commitment which initiated Sunday school efforts. It also promotes the search for methods of action-reflection that will enable the church to be faithful to its vision. Yet it has not clearly demonstrated how these change strategies are to function in contemporary congregations.

Interpretation

Interpretation educators see the task of education as the interpretation of the Christian tradition and the person's present experience in relationship to each other. It is concerned with the way the individual comes to understanding and with the way the individual makes connections among human sciences, personal experience, and world.

While intimations of this approach were seen in the progressive religious education movement, development of the critical tools of hermeneutical and structural analysis was necessary to provide a fully developed approach. The use of tradition in progressive religious education approximates the interpretation approach. Most sophisticated progressive educators were concerned not merely with personal religious needs, as their neo-orthodox critics suggested. Rather, they were concerned with finding a way to link that experience with the living tradition. The University of Chicago educator William Clayton Bower expressed this understanding of Christian education in the 1930s and 1940s.

> Through this approach Christian education becomes a guided experience in facing life situations and in bringing them through to Christian outcomes. The units of learning cease to be blocks of subject matter set in a time schedule and become units of experience undergoing analysis, appraisal and redirection in terms of their potential Christian qualities. In dealing with these experiences the Christian tradition— the bible, Christian thought, the historic development of the church and the rich heritage of symbol and ceremony—

becomes a resource upon which to draw for insights, standards and tested procedures.[30]

Here we see a two-way agenda for Christian education: The theological tradition becomes a source by which experience is made meaningful, and the experience becomes a source for re-making the meaning of the tradition.

More, however, is meant by this process than the oft-spoken dictum "Relate the faith to life." It is the transactions themselves that are the process and content of Christian education—the transactions taking place between person and world, tradition and culture, faith and life. An interpretation educator must ask these questions: What are the meanings derived from daily experience and Christian faith? How are these meanings shaped? Are these meanings "true"? What is the vocation demanded by these meanings? Interpretation is the ongoing process of constructing and testing models that reveal meaning. It attends to the images and intentionalities that direct persons and cultures, and is therefore interested in symbols, rituals, and myths, as well as rational argumentation.

The work of Thomas Groome of Boston College and Douglas Wingeier of Garrett-Evangelical Theological Seminary are illustrative. While they use different theological methods and systems, both are concerned with the process of making connections between personal experience and Christian theology. In their works, one can see that, in the interpretation approach, the process or the transaction is the key. They illustrate that different theological orientations can become the content for the interpretive process. Groome calls his model shared Christian praxis, and Wingeier names his, faith translation.

Groome explains that his approach is interpretive because it "guide[s] people in their attempts to discern God's will for them in their lives and to provide a space within which their discernment can be shared."[31] It recognizes that truth or insight is present both in personal experience and in the Christian story and vision. The individual thus is called to understand the truth, make meaningful connections, and shape a way of living that is faithful to experiences and to tradition. Emphasis is placed equally on personal experience and on the Christian tradition.

Wingeier's approach is interpretive because he seeks to help persons introduce biblical and theological perspectives into the frame of reference by which they normally make sense of their experience.[32] While Wingeier also seeks to understand the points at which faith and human experience intersect, he is much more concerned than Groome with the use of faith as the means of understanding human experience itself—thus the name *faith translation*. In an effort to demonstrate to persons how Christian faith can assist in understanding and decision-making, the movement from faith to life is emphasized over the dialectic relationship between experience and Christian tradition.

Since in these models, the task of Christian education is to instill meaning into both faith and experience, the teacher is not afraid to use the resources of education and the culture, or of socialization and the church, to convey an under-standing of the Christian story; yet this conveying is only one step in a much more complex process which allows the participants "to appropriate the faith tradition critically in their own praxis and . . . to choose further Christian praxis in response to their shared dialogue and reflection."[33] The teacher is more a guide than an instructor or socializer. Groome uses rather poetic terms: The student is a pilgrim who is on a journey, creating history. The teacher is also a pilgrim, but one whose vocation is to guide another on the journey, co-creating history.

Concretely, both Groome and Wingeier suggest an educational process which begins with human experiences. They provide means of assisting the pilgrim in uncovering the interpretive framework through which he or she makes meaning. This framework is thus thrust in tension with the story of the Christian tradition so that the pilgrim can make adequate decisions about faithful belief and faithful living. Interpretation is always the making of meaning from a particular perspective and the re-making of the meaning of that perspective.

Through this process, it is hoped that one can be more sensitive to a personal interpretive framework of meaning—the meaning offered by the culture as well as by the Christian tradition—and the dynamic continuing meaningful revelation of God through life. Interpretation is thus the continuing revision and discovery of patterns of meaning, and it requires that one live faithfully according to the vocation those patterns demand.

The strength of the interpretation position is that it attends to the very transactions through which meanings and models are made. It holistically relates the variables from which Christian education can be built. However, it may fall prey to the same individualistic reductionism as the developmental approach. Without care, the concern for personal knowledge, integration, and meaning may eclipse the transformation demanded by the social situation.

Practical Directions and Implications

While none of these approaches can be found "pure" in the world of Christian education practice, each manifests itself at different times, as decisions about educational goals, curriculum, or teaching strategies are made. These approaches are represented in arguments between those who want to meet the developing needs of the person and those who want to expose that person to social change. They also express themselves in arguments between those who advocate attention to the church's worship and fellowship life because they feel the church's educational program is a waste of time, and those who struggle to make that program the best educational experience possible.

Unless educators can become clear about the metaphors that structure their thinking on the discipline, real conversation is impossible, for persons tend to redefine all conversation through their own position. The following chapters are attempts to uncover these primary metaphors,

CONTEMPORARY APPROACHES TO CHRISTIAN EDUCATION

	Religious Instruction	Faith Community	Spiritual Development	Liberation	Interpretation
Goals	to transmit Christian religion (understandings and practice)	to build the congregation into a community where persons can encounter the faith and learn its life-style	to enable persons to grow in faith to spiritual maturity	to transform the church and persons for liberation and humanization	to connect Christian perspectives and practices to contemporary experiences
View of Teacher	structurer of a learning environment	priest for the community	spiritual director or sponsor	colleague	guide
View of Learner	learner with developmental and personal needs and interests	person struggling to identify with the Christian community; congregation seeking to be faithful	person moving through stages of development to maturity	both "Christian" persons and groups	person seeking to interpret Christianity and experience
Content	Christian religion	Christian community's faith and life-style	Christian faith	critical reflection on life-style in light of Christian faith	Christian story and present experience
Settings for Learning	primarily formal educational settings	community of faith	person's total life	places where Christians are involved in the world	person's total life

Curriculum	teacher structures the learning environment to enable the learner to acquire Christian religion	priest enables congregation to seek to be faithful and exposes "catechumens" to learning points in the community of faith	spiritual director nurtures a person through significant life crises to grow in faith	persons dialogue about their lives so as to bring to awareness structures of power, alternatives for society, and actions for transformation	guide helps persons understand the meaning of experience in relation to the Christian story.
Contribution	serious attention to the application of educational research to the church	increased awareness of the community nature of the Christian church and its educational settings	definition of the ways faith grows in children and adults	concern with the church's mission and involvement in issues of social justice and societal transformation	emphasis placed on discovering relationships among Christian faith, God's present activity, and contemporary experience
Problems	expectation of a higher level of professionalism than may be present in church setting; biased toward more formal educational settings and learning of content	difficulty of intentionally using enculturation structures; apparent assumption that a church community is faithful	difficulty of assessing stages of development; overemphasis on the individual	difficulty of dealing with power and change in the church	difficulty of actually doing theological reflection on experience

translate them into concrete reality, and extend the conversation about an appropriate identity for Christian education.

None of these approaches offers the final answer to the identity for Christian education, but they do provide movement toward it. You are invited to join in the dialogue for that identity.

2

Religious Instruction
Sara P. Little

Religious instruction in this essay is defined as one important part of a total approach to Christian education. While not restricted to any particular setting such as the church school, instruction is thought to permeate the Christian community in actions through which persons explore the church's self-understanding and seek to make it their own. What Sara Little presents here is a theological approach to Christian religious instruction; therefore her statement differs in some respects from the description of religious instruction in chapter 1, which relied upon Christian educators who begin with education instead of with theology. In consonance with her Presbyterian heritage, she emphasizes that right or true thinking is the primary goal of the church's instructional ministry. Such an agenda is concerned that persons come to understand and believe the truth of the faith, so that they may decide to live in ways that are Christian. Therefore the teaching ministry is highlighted as a crucial dimension of church life—a dimension which helps appropriate and recreate the Christian heritage.

My assigned task is to consider religious instruction as one approach to Christian education. Since we are considering the future of Christian education, I assume the editors thought that I thought *instruction* was the single best hope for the future, either as an area of needed reform, or as one that gives promise of so many innovations that a new thing could be brought into existence, or as one that is presently functioning with such perfection that we need only point out existing success.

But I have no zeal for reform, or for innovation, or for complacency—and certainly I cannot imagine myself saying that *any* one idea is *the* best solution or *the* best approach to anything. Why, then, did I accept the invitation? Primarily, I think, to find out what I thought about religious instruction. I have taken at least a small step in that direction, beginning with some ideas I shall continue to explore. The process has necessitated my clearing the way for thinking by stating some presuppositions and by clarifying what I mean by *religious instruction,* first in terms of definition, then in terms of characteristics and functions. Finally, I use the educational categories proposed by Jack Seymour for analysis and summary. You are invited to join in this process, so that we may take the next step together.

Presuppositions

1. *That education is a more comprehensive term than instruction.*

Education includes instruction as one, but only one, of the ways people are educated. In formal terms, education has to do with planned occasions for learning, but it also concerns organizational and administrative practices and resources, and support systems for such activities as instruction. These systems themselves influence people, even by the names of committees and by administrative style. In informal terms, education, though not planned, happens whenever and wherever learning takes place— and that can be anywhere.

When we speak of the future of Christian education, then, we need to discuss more than instruction. We need to talk about long-range strategies and agencies, and about the resultant responsibility of educators. And we must be careful to compare approaches that use categories of the same order.

2. *That the activity called instruction is not to be confused with the setting called schooling.*

Instruction took place when the patriarchs told stories

around campfires as tribes moved from one place to another. Instruction takes place around the table when the Jewish child, at the Passover feast, says, "What is the meaning of this act?" or when a Christian child asks about a television program such as *Roots*, "How could that happen?" Instruction takes place in a business enterprise when a new employee hears, "Do the task this way, not that way" or "This is the reason for our company's policy . . .".

James Michael Lee, one of the best-known interpreters of the religious instruction approach to education, objects to the tendency to equate instruction and schooling: "I am not a proponent of the schooling model, nor have I ever been. Nor am I a proponent of the nonschooling model."[1] Lee is calling for clarity in our use of terminology, a call I endorse.

3. *That religious instruction is only one of the functions that contribute to the purpose of a religious community and that it should be viewed as complementary to, rather than competitive with, those other functions.*

Once I invited a denominational representative to interpret some aspect of a new educational program to one of my classes. After persistent questioning from one member of the class about the evangelistic inadequacies of the program, the speaker stopped, was silent for a moment, then said with just a touch of reprimand in her voice, "I was asked here to talk about education, not about evangelism. That is an important aspect of the life of our church, too, and it is related to education, but it is not education."

When worship is viewed as a major means of education, it becomes something other than the committed response of the Spirit to what one has seen and heard, and is subverted to be other than what, in essence, it is. So with ritual and liturgy. When we engage in mission or ministry in order to teach, rather than to respond as obedient disciples to God's call to faithfulness, then what is learned is something other than what was intended. Indeed, I am tempted to say that every time education becomes imperialistic and tends to take over the whole life and work and worship of the church for its own ends, it is doomed to failure. The same, of course, could be said about *any* one function. When a part becomes the whole, a form of idolatry has emerged. Or to be biblical, I could say that when a part of the body does not fulfill its function, the whole body suffers.

And I do not know which is worse—to be imperialistic or to be so humble and restrained that we do not even see the potential in the task that is given to us.

Religious Instruction

Granted that religious instruction is one, and only one part of a whole; that it is not dependent upon a particular setting; that it is a component in, rather than the equivalent of education—What is it?

To begin, what about the modifier *religious?* For me, it does not mean a particular quality or method of instruction. It simply means that the instruction of which we speak is carried out in the context of a particular religious community and that it takes its orientation from the purposes, language, beliefs, and self-understanding of that community. It is performed by those persons in the community responsible for instruction and therefore focuses on the teacher and on teaching responsibility more than on the student. This is a stipulative rather than a normative designation—a matter of making clear what I mean when I say *religious instruction,* rather than what it ought to mean.

There is a sense in which *instruction* also modifies, or sets limits on, *religious*—or better, *Christian,* since that is the perspective from which this essay is written. One can define instruction in such a way that it means a kind of brainwashing, an unreflective "passing on" of static propositions to be received as correct doctrine. Such a view, admittedly distorted in a negative direction, is one that has caused widespread rejection of even the concept of instruction. I join in such rejection. If *that* is what instruction is, I want nothing to do with it. But as I understand the Christian religion, its very content would prohibit such an approach. That is what I mean by saying that *religious* qualifies *instruction*.

On the other hand, I can gladly affirm such definitions as these selected from the *Oxford English Dictionary:* To instruct means to furnish with knowledge or information; to teach; to educate; to apprise; to inform concerning a particular act or circumstance; to put in order; to form; to inform. There are other suggestions, along with historical comments, but the major thrust of meaning is expressed by the terms I have chosen.

Even more helpful to me in understanding what instruction means is the approach taken by Thomas Green in *Activities of Teaching.* Although Green is considering instruction in the context of general education, I find his view altogether satisfying when used in conjunction with Christian education. For Green, conditioning, training, instruction, and indoctrination—all are activities which can be held to be teaching, to some degree. They include *teaching to* (shaping behavior, as in the realm of skills) and *teaching that* (shaping belief, as in the realm of knowledge). But it is clear that, for Green, instruction is at the heart of teaching.

Green maintains that instruction has to do with those activities that necessitate the "manifestation of intelligence"; that call for concern with the question, Why? It "involves communication *of a certain kind,* and that kind is the kind which includes giving reasons, evidence, argument, and so forth, *for the purpose* of helping another understand or arrive at the truth."[2] In agreement with Green's view, Neely McCarter (now president of Pacific School of Religion) and I once formulated our version of Green's somewhat complicated definition of teaching: Teaching is the process of dealing with subject matter in such a way as to enable students to assess the truth of the same in terms of their own frames of reference.

Several specific observations can be made to relate the concept of instruction to this view of teaching. When one instructs, one deals with the question Why? in relation to what is true, judging from the evidence available to all persons—the "object" sense of "reasonable to believe." But that is not enough. Because teaching is always directed, not to generalized humanity, but to particular persons, the teacher is responsible for helping a student relate what is to be believed to his or her own situation—that is, to deal with the "subject" sense of what is "reasonable to believe."[3] Although he does not state it this way, I believe Green would agree that all kinds of experiences, opinions, human models that influence, and even one's actions, would be factors to be considered in what could be reasonable for a person to believe.

An idea from philosopher H. S. Broudy about types of knowledge offers an additional insight. Although Green is somewhat wary of using the term *knowledge* (his preference is for *belief*), it could be said that from the learner's position, *knowing that* corresponds to Green's *teaching that* and has to do with replicative knowledge—with ideas that can be stored, retrieved, organized, explored. *Knowing how* corresponds only slightly to Green's *teaching to;* it has to do with applicative knowledge, acting, problem solving, and the like. Broudy says we need a third category, *knowing with.* Here he is recognizing contextual knowledge, somewhat similar to Polanyi's tacit knowledge. In addition, *knowing with* could include the developmental context of the person being taught, the tacit knowledge generated by the "paradigms to which Thomas Kuhn alluded in his work on scientific revolutions," and a host of influences assimilated by the person as knowledge.[4] In the final analysis, Broudy says, this *knowing with* may be the most important knowledge of all. From my point of view, I would add that, in the church, we need to be aware of the context in which instruction takes place, use it appropriately, and reflect on it deliberately in connection with our search for what is reasonable to believe.

One final observation—or rather, question. If we take this approach to instruction, essentially that of Green, what happens when we reunite it with *religious?* Religious is still a qualifier, in terms of all types of knowledge. The possibility of contextual knowledge points to the religious community's responsibility to be a community of integrity, where word and deed are consistent. But it is as a *member* of the community that I refer to faithfulness, to worship and service, and to helping build the quality of life that will provide a suitable context for growth into maturity of faith. As *teacher* in this approach to religious instruction, I am intentionally giving my thought, time, and energy to develop those structures and processes within which people can come to understand the gospel. If I am concerned about what is reasonable for the student to believe, I cannot instruct in such a way that *my* version of the gospel must be accepted. I am obviously in agreement at this point with Paul Tillich's comments in his "Question to Christian Ministers and Teachers."

> *How* can the Gospel be communicated? . . . The question *cannot* be: How do we communicate the Gospel so that others will accept it? For this there is no method. To communicate the Gospel means putting it before the people so that they are able to decide for or against it. . . . All that we who communicate this gospel can do is to make possible a genuine decision. Such a decision is one based on understanding and on partial participation.[5]

Tillich's "partial participation" introduces another category we cannot consider here, which has to do with the participation of ministers or teachers in the existence of those with whom they communicate. But the concept of understanding is indeed the goal of the kind of religious instruction we are talking about here. It is a goal which ultimately helps make possible a decision about the gospel.

What, then, is religious instruction? Let me answer the question from the perspective of the Christian community. It is the process of exploring the church's tradition and self-understanding in such a way that persons can understand, assess, and therefore respond to the truth of the gospel for themselves. It can always be the hope, but never the objective of the teacher that the understanding and the assessment will lead to a response that will transform the person as he or she receives the gift of faith.

My inclination now is to begin to state for myself—for us—the meaning of the gospel as I see it, a task which, although appropriate, is not possible here. Such an inclination, however, does suggest that I am talking about a theological approach to religious instruction more than a social-science approach. Thus while I agree with much of James Michael Lee's social-science approach, I can never speak with his confidence about learning outcomes. Indeed, from a theological perspective, I have ethical limitations as to the outcomes I can propose for another person. Because I see that a dialogue between theology and the disciplines of the social sciences can give guidance to the approach to religious instruction that I advocate, I approve of the confessional approach to teaching on occasions when I will not subvert the student's efforts to find what is reasonable to believe. I have no zeal for the professionalizing of teaching. Many volunteer Sunday school teachers, admitting that they do not know, explore with sincerity and diligence the gospel they seek to understand. They explain, too, with clarity sometimes greater than that of those of us who are caught up in the jargon of the day, or who are more concerned with impressing our peers than with being clear. And one last admission. I must agree with Aquinas, commenting on Augustine's views, when he reminds us that it is God who is the teacher and that, in relation to him, we are as farmers or doctors.[6] Like them, we are dependent on him for the final enactment of the task to which we are called. When we speak in this way we are speaking in confessional language, which goes far beyond the "instructional" language that is the emphasis of this paper.

Characteristics and Functions of Religious Instruction

Religious instruction is one of the oldest approaches to education and has undergone so many changes throughout its history that the term evokes many images. In order to be clear about what is meant here, three categories, or key concepts, are established. Each implies characteristics and functions which mark the particular approach we are considering.

1. *Understanding*

A, or perhaps *the* major function of religious instruction, as already suggested, is to encourage the process of thinking, in order that people might understand—understand the gospel and understand themselves and others in relation to the gospel, truth.

Marc Belth, in his *Process of Thinking,* says that "the most basic concern of education is with the deliberate nurturing of the thinking process in each of us."[7] Belth, like Green, is not referring to the accumulating of facts or the storing of propositions that are sometimes called knowledge, although these are appropriate, even necessary activities "on the way to thinking." He is talking about *doing* something with information, including the interpretation of the meaning of experience, and the ordering of information for oneself, and going on to the use of thinking in poetic imagination. My assumption, with Belth, is that one of the distinguishing characteristics of the human being is the ability to think.

Thinking has many functions and takes place in many ways. For Belth, it is closely connected with the way an analogy functions. For Green, it is closely connected to answering the question Why? as one seeks to understand. For Hannah Arendt, it is one of three activities (the other two are willing and judging) which characterize the life of the mind. It has to do with responding to truth, with finding meaning.

Why is it that these authors, and many more in philosophical and general educational circles—though not in religious education—are attending to the idea of understanding? It just may be that, contrary to popular opinion and even to the expressed views of some religious educators, this is a neglected area, and has been for some years. Or it may be that, in our time, the recognition of the desperate need for clear thinking has at last begun to generate concern. Dean Charles Melchert of the Presbyterian School of Christian Education is doing the most significant work that I am aware of in this area, even speaking of education as "helping to understand."[8] It is my hope that many of us will begin to think about understanding as an undertaking crucial to the task of Christian education. I make this statement for many reasons. Let me enumerate only two.

First of all, as people come to acquire the language and the common memory of the religious community of which they are a part, they are thereby engaged in the process of coming to know who they are and what they are for, so as to be able to link their lives to other persons and communities and to ultimate purposes. Many activities can contribute to these same goals—experience, rituals, influences of admired persons, response to human needs or to art, for example. But unless people are in this process of coming to understand, they cannot participate consciously in being responsible for their own lives and for the world in which they live. Another point: Stephen Toulmin, in his philosophical investigation in *Human Understanding*, says that persons are born with the powers of thought—thought which operates "through a particular conceptual inheritance."[9] That inheritance is to be viewed, not as a chain, but as an instrument of thought for recreating the inheritance with each new generation.

Recreating the inheritance is more than a matter of internalizing meaning. It is corporately building each new generation through the activity of the mind, as it adapts the past in novel situations as they emerge, in a kind of "intellectual ecology" which is at the heart of Toulmin's concept of human understanding. Although he is speaking philosophically, his point is applicable for us. For me, Toulmin generates the hypothesis that thinking, directed toward understanding, is the chief activity available to humans to enable us to be intentional about our present and our future. Intentionality thereby becomes one of the key attributes of the kind of understanding that characterizes the approach to religious instruction advocated here.

Second, understanding seeks for, relates to, and is dependent upon what is true. I do not know why, in recent years, more and more I seem to want to say, "Yes, but—what is *true?*" It may be a distrust of that to which we are exposed in media, a fear that we are being manipulated, a disillusionment with institutions. It may be that Kierkegaard's question in *Philosophical Fragments*, "How far does the truth admit of being learned?" is becoming more and more my question. I know that for us humans, truth is never finally learned, but somehow I want to go as far as possible. Kierkegaard's "passion for honesty" humbles me as I think of his fear that he might have acquired a "result" presented to him, rather than appropriated through his own deep struggle to know and respond to truth. I think of a study about education in which it is concluded that "freedom is not permission to flout the truth but to regulate your life in knowledge of it."[10] There are other reflections. The only additional thing I want to say here is that categories of teachers and students vanish at this point. Together, we stand before truth.

Moreover, I know that the careless handling of truth may mean that we become inured to it and to its power for our lives. For teachers, pastors, or educators, the temptation to act as though we are in control of truth, to "manage" it for our purposes, lures us to engage in a potentially self-corrupting activity. The hypothesis generated by such thoughts is that understanding is directed toward, and primarily concerned with, truth. Nothing could be a greater contribution from educators than to focus on that concern for, and in, the Christian community.

2. Deciding

This second category, as I intend to interpret it, may be the one most influenced by the contemporary situation. Although the ability to decide is clearly characteristic of human beings, who are responsible moral agents rather than puppets, it is in our age, specifically, that we hear again and again of the crisis we face. When the Princeton Research Center, on the basis of Gallup polls, concludes that "the U.S. is suffering a moral crisis of the first dimension";[11] when Norman Cousins, Solzenhitzyn, and others say the same thing in different words; and when our own observations confirm such analyses, we wonder what the educational responsibility is. And although I see a general relationship between deciding and understanding, I must thank Hannah Arendt for stimulating me to relate the two to the moral crisis.

In her Clifford Lectures, Arendt comments that her "preoccupation with mental activities" arose from several sources, but especially from her attendance at the Eichmann trial in Jerusalem. There she observed what she calls "the banality of evil." What struck her was the "manifest shallowness of the doer" (Eichmann)—not the demonic nature of his motives, but rather his "mindlessness," or "thoughtlessness." Helpless when routine procedures did not exist to guide his responses, he used "cliché-ridden language" and gave no evidence that he knew how to "stop and think." The question raised for her is this: "Might not the problem of good and evil, our faculty for telling right from wrong, be connected with our faculty for thought?"[12]

Arendt is not saying that thinking is going to solve our problems. She does suggest to me that we should explore the potential in thinking—disciplined, painful, committed thinking—in relationship to our societal problems. If that is the case, one of the tasks of religious instruction is to help persons learn how to use the process of thinking to attack the problems that beset us. And a second task is to move thinking into decision, where we run risks, act, and support one another in our efforts to "do the truth."

Whatever the relationship between the faculty for thought and the problem of good and evil, the question Arendt raises is an intriguing one. Marc Belth, who spends more time on metaphorical thinking than on ethical decision-making, nevertheless sees a connection between thinking and the "profound dilemmas that confront us," although "the dreadful fact about thinking is that it takes time, *and it demands action.*"[13] I would say such action might be "Here I stand," or, "This I must do." Or both. This second task, that of moving thinking and understanding into decision, is one we have only begun to explore.

3. Believing

Even in communities that do not call themselves religious, the kind of instruction Thomas Green talks about is focused on helping persons come to believe—a believing that is informed by pursuit of the question Why? and that is held with both "openness and conviction." That is the same kind of believing I see as the goal of religious instruction. To say the same thing another way, religious instruction is characterized by the activity of helping persons come to believe, always relating that which is reasonable to believe to truth.

Green suggests that teaching might be viewed as the formation and modification of belief systems. At the heart of a belief system are core beliefs, those beliefs "held with such psychological strength" that they "define our most fundamental features of personality."[14] They are the ideas that Ortega y Gasset would say are not "ideas which we *have*, but ideas which we *are*."[15]

Several things should be noted about core beliefs and believing. It is obvious that for Green, believing possesses a dimension of trust, loyalty, and commitment that engages the whole self. But it also contains a strong cognitive component. Wilfred Cantwell Smith, in his polemic in *Belief and History* against the "modern" misuse of the concept of belief as mental assent to a proposition, almost persuades one that belief ought to be discarded as a concern of the religious community. The original biblical meaning, he says, is close to faith. Then in his later *Faith and Belief*, he does make a place for belief as contributing to the reality of faith.

As I see it, *faith* is the religiously important term. The religious community witnesses to the God of truth in every aspect of its life and waits expectantly for the gift of faith. And belief is a factor in faith, either flowing from faith as "faith seeking understanding," or feeding into, deepening, and clarifying faith. To set faith over against belief in debates about focus or purpose of Christian education is to obfuscate the issues.

Are we seeking to develop persons who are clear about everything they believe? Not according to Green. Core beliefs are not easily open to investigation and "ought to enlist our most passionate loyalty, for they are the ones which enable us to hold all other beliefs in a way that leaves them open for instruction and inquiry."[16] The number of core beliefs should be minimized, the clusters of beliefs out nearer the periphery of belief systems should be related to and tested by one another and by core beliefs, and all should be related to the way we act. The *way* beliefs are held, then, is of great importance.

Drawing on other sources, such as sociology and psychology, it seems clear that neither core beliefs nor belief systems will persist unless they are validated in life or perceived as being true; unless they bring clarity and overcome some of the fragmentation that is fostered even by religious institutions, which should serve integrating functions.[17] Further, it is the case that belief is influenced by action, perhaps as much as behavior is influenced by belief.[18] All this is simply to say that when we are talking about believing, we cannot fail to recognize the importance of placing it in the context of all the functions of the church. But as educators, we should focus on the process of understanding as it relates to believing in the context of the community of faith.

Religious Instruction
Analyzed with Educational Categories

The use of Jack Seymour's categories for analysis may pull into focus the implications of this particular approach to religious instruction.

1. *Goals: Appropriation and re-creation for individuals and for the community of the Christian heritage.*

This way of stating the matter should suggest that

"appropriation" involves the development of those core beliefs that are central to the very being of the person. The "re-creation," too, has to do with thinking, understanding, deciding, believing. Otherwise, the community cannot correct its errors, cannot grow in faith and faithfulness. If we depend on socialization alone, reformation would be impossible; we would be limited to the initiation of persons into a community which simply reproduces values, ideas which are not beliefs, empty worship, imitative action. The goal of religious instruction goes far beyond approval of, or entry into, the status quo.

2. *View of the teacher: One who, like the student, stands before the truth; who selects areas for investigation, and structures and processes by which, together, they can ask the question Why?*

For the person envisioned here, *teaching* is not a controlling word, where there can be assured results. But there *is* understanding, and the ability to grow in understanding. To select and structure content and process is an awesome responsibility. And the concept of "standing together before the truth" suggests the kind of mutuality and dialogue so central to Martin Buber's concept of the role of the teacher.

3. *View of the learner: A human being, worthy of respect at every age, born with curiosity and wonder, and needing to receive and respond to the gospel.*

This view is more theological than educational and provides a basis from which a teacher reflects on and utilizes insights from various appropriate disciplines.

4. *Content: The gospel, as it has existed and as it is lived out with deepened meaning, through the formulation and modification of belief systems.*

Actually, there is no "content" that is outside the realm of religious instruction. But the center—the selected, organized beginning point—is the story of God's self-revelation and of human response. Facts and concepts, explored appropriately, move toward the meaning of the gospel.

It is as we think of and plan for the subject matter to be understood that we need to give special attention to contextual knowledge—to the values being communicated through mass media, for instance (e.g., television). The gospel may be distorted so that it is perceived falsely. We need to deal both with the possible use of media for teaching, and with the development of critical skills of analysis as we become aware of what is being communicated.

5. *Settings for learning: Families; the religious community organized for learning, as in the Sunday school; gatherings of the whole congregation; retreats; specialized study support-groups; youth fellowships; church colleges, and so on.*

We are limited here only by our imagination. One of my own thought-ventures for youth has to do with the possibility of periods of residence in campus or conference settings, with carefully structured learning designs, just preceding confirmation. Another has to do with promoting alternative schools and voucher plans, as proposed in a book by James Coleman and others, *Youth: Transition to Adulthood.* There are others. They draw on the school setting, but are not limited to it, nor do they modify it substantially. In any event, I do not find schooling a "bad word." I agree with Locke Bowman's judgment that schools are not "the monstrous deterrents to faith development" that some religious educators suppose.[19]

6. *Curriculum: The intentional selection and arrangement of materials and learning strategies in relation to purpose, persons, situations, and context.*

The key word here is "intentional." If a teacher's intention is to involve the class in an interactive process where both instructional and personally nurturing values are sought, he or she will take a certain approach. If the intention is to transmit subject matter or to develop information or concepts, he or she will focus on developing strategies most appropriate for information-processing. If the intention is to help class members become involved in identification with the perspectives, attitudes, and values of others, or to emphasize aspects of self-understanding and personal growth, the teacher will select activities such as simulation to facilitate the goal. *Models of Teaching*, by Bruce Joyce and Marsha Weil, is extremely helpful in enabling teachers to see the range of options available and to learn that there is no one best way to teach. Another approach, one particularly useful in church education, is to develop learning strategies around types of knowledge and ways of knowing, a project on which Neely McCarter and I have worked together for a number of years.[20] The Christian Education Shared Approaches (CE:SA) plan might be said to have begun to explore the concept of intentionality, although one major rationale for that idea was to meet the theological and educational pluralism that exists in the church.

7. Contribution: Helping persons come to know what they believe, as they recreate and live out their heritage.

The need for clarity of belief (held in openness and conviction) is great at this moment in history. Ortega y Gasset says that "people can handle almost anything life hands them *except* not being clear" about what they believe.[21] If we are a people who indeed are characterized by a kind of "homelessness of mind," as sociologist Robert Bellah says, we should give attention to the way beliefs and belief systems are formed and held. That seems to be a concern distinctively characteristic of the responsibility of the teaching ministry.

8. Problems: Distorted images and misinterpretation of the past, faddism, search for forms and methods that will "work" with little effort, failure to think clearly.

There are other problems, of course, such as the elusive and complex problem of knowing how to deal with religious instruction when it is so dependent on the context in which it exists, the quality of life in the community in which it is developed, and the awareness of the mission of that community. But even these difficulties are outweighed by the possibilities present in this approach.

Other interpretations of religious instruction would call for different statements in each category. But the pervasive, unifying theme of religious instruction is the affirmation of the processes of understanding, deciding, and believing, as they impinge upon engagement with and response to the gospel. And there is a renewed call to make teaching ministry an integral part of the total life of the church. There is more to the teaching ministry than religious instruction, but religious instruction is at the heart of teaching.

3

The Faith Community As a Guiding Image for Christian Education

Charles R. Foster

A theological description of the Christian community of faith is proposed as the foundation for Christian education. In terms of practice, Charles Foster illustrates how the natural means of Christian stories, roles, and symbols— the means by which the faith community transmits its faith and life-style from one generation to another—become the primary means for Christian education. Yet in his description, he transcends some of the difficulties of other faith community educators by considering the fact that the American context for the church is one of voluntarism, where persons choose to which churches they will go, and to what degree they will participate. He illustrates that a crucial task for the Christian educator is to attend to the way a voluntary community is built and maintained. The faith community approach in a stable Christian environment looks very different from the way it appears in a plural religious environment.

A few short years ago Alex Haley reminded us of the social and historical character of the human experience.[1] In searching for his own roots back through the experience of slavery to the African continent, he revealed the power of our often unconscious bonds with unknown ancestors and distant places. He illustrated the interplay of our various histories in his exploration of the meaning of his own ancestors' experience. He demonstrated the fact that the story of neither the black nor the white experience in this country can be told in isolation. Each is necessary to the understanding of our respective pasts as well as our contemporary interdependence. It is this corporate sense of the human experience—reflected in Haley's quest and exceeding the limits of our finite memories and visions—that I wish to spotlight in my use of the community of faith as a guiding image for our work in Christian education.

What Is a Community of Faith?

It is a people whose corporate as well as personal identities are to be found in their relationship to some significant past event. Their reason for being may be traced to that event. Their response to that event shapes their character, confirms their solidarity, and defines their identity. Their unity is expressed through their commitment to that event, and their destiny is revealed in the power of its possibilities. A community of faith may be organized around any past event. From a Christian perspective, however, the formative power of an event takes place through the initiative of God. The originating event for all human history took place in the act of Creation. It has been renewed subsequently in those times and places where persons have experienced that same creative power in redemptive form. The community takes shape through the accumulating responses of men and women to God's continuing action.

In the biblical record we may discern the formation of a community of faith in the response of persons to the stories about Abraham and Sarah. These stories focus upon a man and woman who, at the call of God, risked leaving their homeland. In the repetition of their response through their descendants, they became known as the father and mother of the people of the Promised Land. That event—their following God to an unknown destination—located the people in a place. It identified them as the people of Yahweh. It gave them a vision of their destiny among the nations of the world. The power of that event may still be seen in the intensity of the identification of the Jewish people with that place. To the extent that we who call ourselves Christian are committed to the originating power of such Old Testament events, we may share the experiences of those identified with them. With the apostle Paul, we too may look back upon Abraham and Sarah as our spiritual ancestors.

Many other events have served to remind people of the creative power of God. The Exodus, the Exile into Babylon, the rebuilding of Jerusalem following the Exile—these are a few of the all-encompassing events through which the people of God have clarified and renewed their relationship to each other, to their neighbors, and to the source of their being.

The formative event for the corporate and personal identities of Christians comes from our relationship to the responses of persons through the ages to the action of God in the life, death, and resurrection of Jesus Christ. We sometimes symbolize that relationship by calling ourselves the people of the cross. That instrument of torture and death serves to remind us of an event which, paradoxically, reveals for us the source and purpose of life.

We describe who we are in relation to the cross. We call ourselves the Body of Christ. We are Christians. Through the cross, we describe the interdependence of the human race. We speak of loving our neighbors as we have been loved—even to the point of ultimate sacrifice. We give form to the continued experience of that event through rituals and traditions. We have created institutions to make that continuity possible. And we seek to preserve its power in our lives through the use of ancient creeds and by retelling old stories. At the same time we attempt to claim the event's creative power for the present by reinterpreting it in light of new circumstances; using contemporary modes of communication, we recreate it. Discerning our destiny in that event, we respond to its intent by striving for justice. We extend the compassionate concern of Jesus to the dispossessed and despised. We minister to the sick and lonely. As commitment to the Christ-event becomes the organizing center for our lives, it also becomes the focus of our personal and corporate identities.

We experience this corporate identity of the Christian community in at least three ways. In the first place, *we know we are Christian because we participate in Christianity's historical embodiment.* Our ties to the ancestors of this community are stronger than the linear sequence of relationships described by a series of "begats" or a genealogy chart. They partake of the intimacy of the relationship that links ancient and contemporary participants in the corporate response to the power of a common formative event. This earthy and primordial experience is perhaps best conveyed through the words of a spiritual: Rocking my soul in the bosom of Abraham. When we sing this line, we participate, as Carl Jung has emphasized, in the corporate phenomenon of being human. We are drawn back into the most significant of all formative interactions between parent and child— touching, holding, protecting, sustaining. It is through these elemental experiences that persons learn to trust the world around them.

Our historical relationship to the formative events in our corporate lives has a special meaning in this discussion. I do not refer to the intellectual disciplines which distinguish, distance, and make discrete the relationship of past and present, but to those experiences that create a sense of immediacy between our present and our past. By historical, I mean our participation, primarily in unconscious fashion, in the depths of the human experience. Through the use of rituals and symbols, and often in the midst of play, these resources of that unknown past come welling up into our words and actions to reveal our interdependence with the total human experience. This historical perspective grounds our identity and provides the framework for exploring who we are and what we are about.

Our corporate identity, moreover, is experienced relationally. It is caught up in institutional structures, customs, and kinship networks. It bonds persons into relationships across time and space.

From a Christian perspective, a person exists only in

relationship to others. This theme is not only the key to the Creation stories' emphasis on the interactions between God and his human creations; it is also central to their emphasis on the interdependence of man and woman for their personal well-being as well as for the future of the race. And it is at the very heart of what we, over the centuries, have called the good news. It is only in the gathered fellowship that the presence of Christ is revealed. It is in serving others that we see, hear, and feel the healing and redeeming presence of God in Christ.

The significance of bonding relationships is asserted most sharply, perhaps, by Erik Erikson. His thesis is that trust is the foundation for all other developmental learning tasks. He contends that trusting relationships from early childhood onward are essential to personal spiritual growth. Trust enables us to take risks. It invites us to explore the unknown. It allows us to recognize and affirm our finitude without undue anxiety. It frees us to engage in that reciprocity of giving and receiving upon which all human interacton is based.

Martin Buber, in the course of his discussion on the interdependence of an "I" and a "Thou," calls attention to the way all our relationships with others are forever caught in the tension between the pull into intimacy and the push into isolation. This push and pull is given order in the institutions we create to perpetuate the customs and mores which facilitate our communication with one another. These structures assure and enhance the continuity of our communication and make visible our interdependence.

The identity of the community is also experienced spontaneously. The paradigm for such events may have taken place at Pentecost. It is reflected in our use of the words *celebration* and *happening* to describe occasions that exceed the bounds of the expected. Victor Turner has called this expression of community *communitas* to distinguish its experience from the structures of community usually explored by social scientists. Robert Evans has observed that *communitas* never can be created, structured, or willed into existence. *Communitas* can only be celebrated. It is not a "possession."

It is a "gift." It is not a state, but a moment. It is "Not segmented; it is wholistic. It is not hierarchical, but . . . egalitarian."[2] Participants are not known to one another by their roles, jobs, or positions, but in the commonality of their submission to the power of the moment. In these spontaneous moments of community we experience the spaciousness of time, the intimacy of the transcendent, and the transformation of the immediate. The usual social distinctions of race, age, social and economic class, or geography fade from consciousness. We experience one-ness. It is the function of *communitas* to intensify community, render solidarity, and renew vision.

The spontaneous moments in which our corporate identity is revealed cannot be structured. But they occur in and through the structures that provide continuity and form for our existence. Such moments remind us of who we are. They renew our commitments to the source of our corporate life. They may also transform that collective memory for the future. During Pentecost, for example, the past was not only recalled and renewed; it was relived in a new way. We often refer to the newness of that event as the birth of the Church. It was not a private event, but a public event—linking past and future in the present.

Implications for Christian Education

Thanks in particular to the work of C. Ellis Nelson and John Westerhoff, the insights and categories of sociology and anthropology have come to be increasingly explored and appropriated by Christian educators.[3] They have called our attention to the fact that the life of a congregation and its larger cultural milieu influence the content and character of a person's faith commitments as much as, if not more than, the educational programs of a given congregation. They have similarly made us aware of the socializing patterns at work in the transmission of values and practices from the older to the younger members of a congregation; the pervasive influence of what Westerhoff has called the "hidden curriculum" in any social organization; as well as the persistence of certain liturgies, rituals, rites of passage, and traditions in filling out the content of the faith commitments of persons. In short, they have sensitized us to how greatly the social disposition of the human enterprise is reflected in the essentially corporate and communal character of the church's efforts to incorporate ever-new generations of children and youth into its life and mission. When one considers the community of faith as a significant guiding image for our work in Christian education, its corporate perspective dominates the categories we use and the procedures we choose.

Purposes of Christian Education

Perhaps the most basic clue for the purpose of Christian education from a "community of faith" perspective occurs in Paul's first letter to the Corinthians. In the midst of his discussion of the gift of the Spirit and the primacy of love among the virtues to be nurtured, Paul urges the members of the Corinthian congregation to contribute their gifts in the worship of God, to the end that the church might be built up. To "build up" does not mean simply to acquire new members. It involves nurture, instruction, interpretation, ecstatic utterance, hymn-singing, and sustenance and support. Its emphasis is corporate, not individual; personal, rather than private. Its focus is not upon the members of the congregation, but upon God. Several goals for the educational ministry of our churches may be discerned in the challenge "to build up the church."

Congregations committed to this task will seek first to hand on to the next generation their appropriation of the event from the past which identifies who they are and what their destiny entails. They will consciously strive to make the people, circumstances, and consequences of that event accessible to all who enter the life of the Christian community under their auspices. They will also provide opportunities for those persons to explore the implications of the accrued meanings from that event for use in their own experience.

Congregations committed to this task will, in the second place, undertake to transmit the life-styles that identify them as members of the Christian community. The popular hymn, "They Will Know We Are Christians by Our Love," reflects this goal of Christian education. It involves the shaping of attitudes and behavior so that the content of the community's commitments might be revealed in the relationships and decisions of their daily lives, from one generation through the next.

Third, congregations committed to this task will recreate the organizing event for the ever-new context in which people find themselves. It is not the task of Christian education simply to replicate and perpetuate. The church educates, among other reasons, in order to be able to update its resources from the past. Just as Second Isaiah was called to reinterpret Israel's sense of destiny out of the humiliation of defeat and exile, today's church is challenged to incorporate into its appropriation of past events the meanings emerging from our contemporary situation.

View of the Teacher

The urgency to teach is rooted in the community's commitment to the values of its past, for the sake of its future. At this point Westerhoff has been helpful. He rightly insists that the whole life of the community teaches. The task of teaching cannot be limited to specific times and places. Any person who regards the life and commitments of the community as important may well end up teaching others in formal as well as informal settings. The community-wide acceptance of the responsibility to teach may be seen in the common learning of new hymns or, for that matter, in the efforts of a long-time member to help a visitor make use of the hymnal during worship. It is evident, too, when an adult stops two children in the midst of a personal scuffle to discern what is taking place and to give suggestions for resolving their problem. It is also apparent whenever a child takes an adult by the hand to see the picture a class painted to illustrate one of the parables of Jesus. And it may be observed in the repetition of certain rituals central to the way a given congregation worships, helps others, and gives order to its daily decisions.

But the commitment to exploring and opening up the past is too important to be left to chance encounters. The community of faith is dependent upon designated as well as undesignated teachers—persons who deliberately tell the stories of the people, who consciously explore the implications of past events for contemporary decisions, and who professionally seek to interpret current events in the light of the community's heritage, both for those entering the community and for those moving to a new stage or role in its life.

Teachers are engaged in a dialogical activity. On the one hand, they represent the community in activating learning, and as such, they are responsible to the values and the intent of the community's experience. And if they are to be effective, they must be sensitive to the capacities, needs, and interests of those who are learners. Not only do teachers bridge the gap between the resources of the community and the learners, who need those resources in order to participate in the corporate life with purpose, meaning and power; they serve, at the same time, as mediators between the past-oriented members of the community and the learners, who bring with them distinctive perceptions, experiences, and abilities which the community needs to extend its life and mission into the future.

The dialogical character of teaching and learning in the community of faith is especially evident in the fluid manner in which the teachers and learners exchange roles. The learners organize their experience in quite personal ways. Their grasp of meanings and practices occurs in the context of their own situations. When they reveal the meanings they have appropriated from the teacher's efforts, they may well introduce the teacher to a new angle of vision on a familiar theme. This new insight may, in turn, alter the teacher's own viewpoint. In other words, in the interplay between past events and future possibilities, both teachers and learners are exposed to new ideas and insights.

The commitment of the community of faith to its past is reflected in the urgency with which it seeks out its teachers and the high regard with which it views them. They are more than classroom managers and facilitators of learning. Their function is more than technical. They are not interested in value-free patterns of education. They are concerned with incorporating an ever-new generation of persons into the membership of the community. Their task culminates in commitments to the destiny of the community emerging out of its originating event. It is in the urgency to teach and in the self-conscious support of teaching that a community of faith may sustain its commitments in an increasingly pluralistic society.

Teachers in the community of faith have several distinct responsibilities. They introduce students to the stories which illumine the identity and destiny of the community; they establish the context and perceptual screen through which contemporary experiences might be perceived, understood, interpreted, and appropriated. And they repeat these stories until they become a part of the student's imaginal reservoir for thinking and acting.

They instruct persons in the ways the community perceives, thinks, and acts, that they may participate in the life of that community. James Michael Lee has pointed out that instruction has to do with life-style. From this perspective, teachers instruct so that there might be continuity in the values and commitments, the decisions and actions of past and future generations. Their task, in other words, involves the continuity of the cultural expression of the people.

As a link between past and future in the corporate experience of the community, teachers update historic values, commitments, and practices as they respond to the demands of contemporary events and circumstances. The past is appropriated—not blindly, but with an awareness of both the continuities and the discontinuities between our ancestors' encounters and our own encounters with our mutual heritage.

As a link between past and future, teachers assess the

responses we make to contemporary events in the light of historic values and commitments. Teachers critique, if you will, our attitudes, decisions, and actions in an effort to discern the extent to which they have maintained the integrity of the originating events in the community's life. They refuse to allow us to fall into traps of generality, platitude, and vagueness. They engage us with the particularity of what we do and of its relationship to the source and destiny of our corporate life.

View of the Learner

A community of faith perspective assumes that all persons in the community, regardless of age, sex, social, racial, economic, or other cultural distinctions, are learners. They are learners by virtue of their membership in the community, whether they entered it through birth, conversion, or immigration. There may well be differences in the status persons enjoy as learners, but there is no difference in their basic relationship to the community itself.

Learning is a lifelong process, not relegated to a given period of life. One of the more helpful images of the learner, from our perspective, is that of the pilgrim on a journey marked by different stages and changing status. The pilgrimage is not necessarily linear, sequential, or progressive. Some pilgrims stop at way stations and proceed no farther. Others retreat from their destination—a phenomenon many call backsliding. This retreat may be masked by occasional bursts of energy and long periods of quiescence. The pilgrimage does entail changing roles, all related to the extent to which the member-learner identifies with and reveres the intent and destiny of the community's life. These changing roles may entail movement from member of a family in the community, to baptized member, to confirmed member, to called member with designated responsibilities, to wise member, to honored or revered member. Each of these changes in the person's relationship to the life of the community reintroduces the member-learner to the experience of the novitiate or apprentice.

Persons who are beginners in a new relationship require the counsel, guidance, and experience of those who are able to introduce them to the events and meanings from the past, with the freshness and vitality of their "new" positions.

Content for Teaching and Learning

The life of the community is the content of Christian education. Participation in its heritage, rituals, traditions, and life-styles, as well as its thinking, values, and institutions provides both the context and the content of the interaction between teachers and learners. The task is not to learn about, but to engage in that life. The content of teaching is not abstracted from the circumstances of daily experience; it is rather the ongoing dialectic between that which has been received and that which is encountered from both the natural and social environments.

In a Christian community of faith, the content necessarily involves the interaction of God with all humanity. The life of the community embodies the responses of all persons to the initiating activity of God throughout human history. We refer to this action as the work of creation, redemption, and judgment. By contemplating it, we are able to discern the contrast between our human shortcomings and the patience of God's sustaining love. We are then driven first, to confess our inability to be faithful and next, to celebrate our experience of forgiveness and liberation.

Since the content of Christian education in the community of faith involves the remembering, reliving, and recasting of that ancient relationship, teaching may occur at any point in the life of the community. Teaching may occur, in other words, whenever members of the community seize the opportunity to explore the God/human relationship in the worship, fellowship, study, mission, or administration of the congregation.

Settings for Teaching and Learning

In the community of faith, the place for teaching and learning is not as important as the interaction between teacher and student. Perhaps this is the reason John

Westerhoff has tended to play down the significance of the "school" in the development of faith. The importance of such interaction is clearly evident in the teaching of Jesus. He told stories, instructed his listeners in the way of God, and interpreted the meanings of events and relationships whenever he found people ready to hear him. Contemporary settings similarly may involve any place or program in the life of the congregation. It may occur in homes, on the streets, in social and service clubs, on radio or TV—wherever and whenever pilgrims and a guide may happen to meet.

This is not to deny the value of a "school" for teaching and learning. But it is to challenge the necessity of the structure of the school as we know it, with its sequence often unrelated to capacity or interest; with its tendency to approach teaching and learning as nonreciprocal activities; with its inclination to function over against the life of the community rather than as an integral part of it; and finally, with its emphasis upon control rather than liberation. Teaching in the community of faith requires programs and structures that make it possible for people to develop the skills and achieve the wisdom that will enable them to participate in its life responsibly and creatively. These structured settings—schools if you will—help ensure the continuity of the community's commitments to its own heritage and destiny.

The most effective settings for teaching and learning are to be found where people are engaged in exploring their relationship to the values and commitments of the community, particularly when the identity of the community and its members is being challenged and tested by internal confusion and discord or by external pressures and threats. Such an opportunity exists, for example, when a predominantly middle-class congregation finds itself in the midst of a rapidly changing neighborhood. Again, it presents itself whenever persons are prepared to participate in the rituals and rites of passage of the congregation. Although such events embody corporate expectations, they nevertheless leave room for quite personal responses. That is true also of the daily decisions and actions in the conduct of family, vocational, or civic responsibilities, which offer still other openings for teaching and learning. Church school classes, the homes of church members, worship services, mission projects, hospital visits, and even chance encounters on the street—all these places and occasions are settings for teaching and learning. They become significant for the educational ministries of the church as soon as persons acknowledge their potential for transmitting and renewing the faith. The school of the community of faith occurs, in other words, whenever and wherever teachers engage others as learners and learners engage others as teachers.

Curriculum in the Community of Faith

I would like to discuss curriculum through the use of a simple scheme which, I hope, will make visible several obvious implications for the content of teaching and learning in congregations which employ the assumptions of a community of faith perspective in their work.

The first and most basic component in such a curriculum may be found in the remembered and printed accounts of the events in the community's life in which the purpose and will of God has been discerned and celebrated, and the faithfulness of the responses of the persons involved has been identified and affirmed. These accounts are found in stories, songs, and creeds. We place special emphasis upon those found in the Bible, since it functions as the primary source for all our teaching and learning. Its significance is revealed in the way the Christian community of faith has often looked upon itself as the "people of the Book." Our identity and mission are found in the content of our commitment to the framework it establishes for our lives. The creeds, stories, and hymns of the church reveal the continued activity of God in the history of humanity and underscore the relevance and liveliness of the original stories. They provide the sources for our own engagement with the God of Creation and the Lord of history, here and now.

A second component in a community of faith curriculum consists of the composite of resources developed by that community to remind itself of its identity, to identify persons in its life and mission, and to interpret its experience in light of its heritage. The formal prayers, liturgies, creeds, oratorios, artistic creations, and theological interpretations make it possible for persons to encounter, explore, and appropriate significant community meanings and practices. When we look back over the curricular resources of most Protestant churches during this century, we discover that most of them were drawn from this ecclesiastical treasury.

A third component is to be found in the structures, relationships, and traditions of the community of faith itself. These are the elements of the "hidden curriculum" of which Westerhoff speaks. They may either reinforce or undermine the formal teaching of the community. They may be consciously perpetuated. Or they may, unwittingly, reflect the values of the larger society in which the community exists. It is this curricular component that congregations most often ignore in their evaluations of the faithfulness of their educational ministries in light of their understanding of the good news. In a society influenced by the assumptions of voluntarism, the significance of this component of curriculum will not go unexamined by any community of faith bent on squaring its actions with its words. The task of clarifying the relationship of the structures and values of a congregation to those of the larger society is, of course, a never-ending one. It demands of us an ever-growing consciousness of the socializing process at work in the community as it influences the relationship of the commitments and behavior of its members.

For Further Consideration

The strengths of an educational ministry guided by the image of the community of faith are obvious. It would regard as significant the corporate experience of being human and the interdependent character of our common life. It would use the resources of the past to open up the possibilities of the future. In the process, it would affirm the importance of teachers and learning for all persons. It would lend itself readily, moreover, to the interplay between the events of teaching and learning and the events of celebration and mission.

An educational ministry guided by a communal image embodies several inherent potential limitations, as well. The corporate emphasis may be easily distorted into a preference for the status quo. The emphasis upon history may deteriorate into a nostalgic fascination for a limited past. The stress upon teaching may lead some to forget that learners appropriate and integrate their experience in relation to their capacities and situation. This lapse often has led teachers to redirect their efforts—from opening up the resources of the community for learners to controlling the responses of learners.

Each of these strengths and limits could be discussed at length. In this brief space, however, I would rather identify a problem that anyone interested in the communal emphasis of this approach to Christian education must face. This problem has become evident to me as I have read and reread the works of John Westerhoff, who is undoubtedly the best-known proponent of the community of faith approach. Westerhoff has focused upon and illumined many of the issues central to my own thoughts about Christian education. And yet I find that one persistent question keeps me from following his increasing tendency to merge the tasks of liturgy and education, to reduce the distinction between priest and teacher, and to deemphasize the significance of some form of "schooling."[4] That question is simply this: Is it possible to make use of the corporate and historical imagery of the community of faith in a society governed by the assumptions and expectations of voluntarism? On the surface, at least, communal and voluntary approaches to social organization are often contrary. In this brief space, it is all too easy to exaggerate the distinctions between the voluntary and the communal perspectives. Yet their differences are too important for us not to take note of them. Whereas the voluntary tends to view the flow of time in linear, sequential, and progressive patterns, the communal emphasizes the interplay of the continuities of the past with the emergence of the new. Whereas the voluntary is exclusive, the communal is inclusive. Then most important of all, whereas the voluntary assumes a consensus of values in the larger culture, allowing for a wide variety of specific institutions with clearly defined goals and procedures, the communal assumes a diversity of values in the larger culture, given common meaning and purpose in overarching institutions, creeds, rituals, and traditions.

This last point can be made in another way. Leaders in voluntary societies rarely view as important what I have called the historical sources for our corporate identity. They focus primary attention on what is consciously known, and on procedures that might create and sustain the bonds of freely chosen relationships, which also may be freely severed. Leaders concerned with more communal social structures, on the other hand, tend to do exactly the opposite. They stress the significance of those rituals, rites, and traditions which evoke the historical expression of their corporate life.

Voluntary assumptions have dominated the way we as a nation have organized our political, social, economic, and, among Protestants in particular, religious concerns; in fact, much of the rhetoric and many of the programmatic decisions of Roman Catholics indicate their growing acceptance of many of these assumptions. In recent years, however, I have discerned a shift in the voluntary character of our society. The old centrist Protestant concerns which once undergirded our various political, educational, ecclesiastical, and economic institutions no longer exist. That collapse may be most visible in the almost frenetic, but selective appeal of prominent politicians and religious personalities to the values and structures of an earlier period in our national history. It is evident, as well, in the dissipation of such national rituals as the Fourth of July into a family vacation. It is apparent also in the way many congregations draw the connection—or fail to draw the connection—between the God of Creation and their stewardship of resources; between the Lord of all nations and their loyalty to this nation; and between the Christ of history and their support of a narrow nationalistic view of the mission of America in the world. It can be seen, too, in the growing numbers of persons who are abandoning a Judeo-Christian world-view to commit themselves to the formative power of events clustered around Buddha, Muhammad, or some contemporary religious leader.

This collapse in the consensus undergirding the voluntary character of our social and political structures has not reduced our national commitment to voluntary presuppositions. On the contrary, it has seemed only to reinforce and intensify their importance for many. This situation creates enough problems for the Christian educator who is guided by the assumptions of voluntarism. For the Christian educator who is seeking to implement strategies based on corporate assumptions, the difficulties may seem overwhelming. The task however is an important one. The distinctive contribution of those Christian educators who are guided by an image of the community of faith is the underscoring of the importance of the historical and corporate character of the educational ministry of the church. These emphases provide an important antidote to the tendency of voluntary societies to ignore the interdependence of humanity.

Summary

The community of faith is one guiding image for our work in Christian education. It emphasizes the corporate character of the human experience in which personal identity is grounded in the commonality of being human. It views the past as the springboard for the present and future. It regards the educational ministries of the church as the responsibility of the whole people of God. At the same time, it emphasizes the function of teaching as an urgent expression of its concern to incorporate into its life the children of an ever-new generation, through whom its corporate destiny might continue to be explored and lived out. As a guiding image for our work in Christian education, the community of faith focuses upon tasks central to building up the church, that God might be worshiped and glorified.

4

The Developmental Approach to Christian Education

Donald E. Miller

The historic and constructive relationship between developmental psychological theory and Christian education is described in this chapter. While the work of significant developmental theorists is summarized and implications are drawn for the theory and practice of Christian education, Donald Miller reminds us of the limitations and problems that arise when connecting developmental theory and Christian education. He particularly questions the cultural and historical bias of the theories and their understandings of transformation and conversion. Significant for the Christian educator is his expansion of the notion of development beyond the individual's personal process of growth into a dynamic interaction of individual and community. The necessary relationship between the developmental and the faith community theories is thus illustrated.

The twentieth century has seen the concept of development move to the center of the Christian education movement. Horace Bushnell, in the mid-nineteenth century, gave a powerful statement of the need for development in Christian education when he wrote that children should never know themselves not to have been Christian.[1] He was fighting against the efforts of child evangelists to convince children of their sin and convert them to Christianity. Bushnell objected to children being treated as adults and called for materials that were appropriate to their level of maturity. This concern for graded materials was met at the turn of the century in the same decade as the founding of the Religious Education

Association. Much of the effort of religious educators in the twentieth century has gone toward the production of age-related materials. Our task in what follows is to reassess the concept of development for the future of religious education.

The concept of development in education is certainly not without precedent in previous centuries, even though it was given enormous impetus in the wake of Darwin by the power of the theory of cultural evolution. The Scriptures often suggest a roughly developmental sequence to life. "When I was a child, my speech, my outlook, and thoughts were all childish. When I grew up, I had finished with childish things" (I Cor. 13:11). Or again, "I had to deal with you on the merely natural plane, as infants in Christ. And so I gave you milk to drink, instead of solid food, for which you were not yet ready" (I Cor. 3:1b-2). A more powerful expression is given in Ephesians 4:13: "So shall we all at last attain to the unity inherent in our faith and our knowledge of the Son of God—to mature manhood, measured by nothing less than the full stature of Christ."

The concept of development is also found in Greek and Roman literature. Plato proposed an educational curriculum which moved from the chimera of sense experience to the eternal reality of form.[2] Education was a matter of leading persons away from an exclusive reliance upon sense experience, to an awareness of the eternal realities. Children were to study fables, poetry, and music—popular arts that are dominated by sense experience. Athletics came next, followed by arithmetic and astronomy, subjects less dominated by sense experience and close to formal principles. Finally by age thirty, a person was ready to study philosophy and be led to appreciate purely formal reality. By thirty-five, one was prepared to follow an occupation; and by fifty, to give service to the state.

Much educational literature in the ancient and medieval periods made little effort to adapt to the growing capacities of children. *Aesop's Fables* are no exception, in that they originally were for adults and only later were published for children. Sensitive educators continued to call for a concept of development. On this basis, Rousseau scathingly criticized religious education as he saw it practiced.

> But though a child should profess the Christian religion, what can he believe? He can believe only what he conceives, and he conceives so little of what is said to him, that if you tell him directly the contrary, he adopts the latter dogma as readily as he did the former. The faith of children and indeed of many grown persons, is merely an affair of geography.[3]

The great significance of John Newbery's *Mother Goose's Nursery Rhymes* was that they were printed simply because they were delightful to young children. The *New England Primer* was a carefully graded approach to moral education, under the premise that contemplation of dying was the beginning of wisdom for children as well as for adults. McGuffey's *Reader* was in the same tradition, leading the child through a graded sequence of biblical and moral selections, though not with such Puritan emphasis. *Alice in Wonderland* is so important because it was written as a fantasy, expressly for children, by a gifted logician. These efforts have culminated in a great focus upon "development" in the religious education of the twentieth century.

The Concept of Development

Three basic elements in the concept of development are listed by R. S. Peters: a preexisting structure, an invariant sequence, and an end-state.[4] Careful consideration will, in my judgment, lead us to add two other elements: integration of increasingly complex elements, and interaction between individual and environment. A ground plan, an invariant sequence, and a final purpose can result merely in progress without development. A meal, a race, or an afternoon outing contains all three elements, but only if there is the integration of increasingly complex elements, and only if there is definable interaction, can we speak of their developing. The prototype of development is the living organism. Personalities and groups develop by analogy to organisms.

The idea of development need not be limited to the individual—groups, communities, and nations also develop. In Christian education, development usually applies to individuals, but such limitation is not necessary to the concept. I will accept the limitation of referring to the religious development of individuals, since others have taken on the task of the community as educator, but I will argue that the development of an individual is always in relation to a network of environing communities.

Development always presumes a ground plan, or what R. S. Peters calls a "pre-existing structure."[5] For Freud, the ground plan is that every individual moves through oral, anal, and genital stages. Piaget's ground plan is that each person moves through sensorimotor, preoperational, concrete operational, and formal operational stages. But of this, more in a moment. Suffice it to say that development presumes some ground plan or structure through which every individual moves.

Closely related to the ground plan is the idea of invariable sequence. Any given stage presumes the previous stage and leads to the next stage. In Piaget's account, a child cannot think concretely and literally until it has passed through the preoperational stage of mythical thinking. Furthermore, no stage can be skipped. A child cannot move from sensorimotor skills directly to concrete thinking without passing through the stage of preoperational thought. An individual can move through the sequence either quickly or slowly and, indeed, may be arrested in development at a given stage. Difficulties in one stage may cause difficulties in a later stage. In Erik Erikson's account, failure to establish basic trust in the first year of life may cause serious problems in all succeeding stages.

Development contains a third dimension—the integration of increasingly complex elements. All things are the result of what has gone before, but the concept of development presumes that an individual achieves a dynamic unity of existing elements. Whereas on one hand the integration represents a universal stage, on the other, it also represents a unique synthesis by the individual. This synthesis will remain stable until challenged by elements that will not fit, at which time the individual is driven through a period of crisis toward a new integration. Let us consider again Erikson's description of the infant's first year. The growing capacities of the child and the increasing independence from the parent lead to a crisis of trust, the established relationship to the parent being tested by the new independence. The child must integrate the need for autonomy into a personal pattern and is thereby thrust into a new stage.

A fourth element of development is the interaction between the individual and the environment. It is difficult to imagine a development that is not interactional with the environment. For persons, interaction with the physical environment will give a sense of reality; interaction with the social and cultural environment will give a sense of selfhood and responsibility. Anyone who insists upon a noninteractional view of development will come out with a much different conclusion.

A fifth and final element of the concept of development is that of a particular goal, or *telos*. Development does not just terminate; rather it moves toward some final level of complex integration, which is usually referred to as maturity. Of all the elements in the concept of development, perhaps maturity is the most difficult to define. In a process view, maturity is the openness of the individual to move to the next stage. In an end-state view, maturity is the final stage before the dissolution of the individual. The ambiguity between the process and end-state views of maturity often confuses discussion of the concept of development.

Cognitive Development

Religious education in the twentieth century has been influenced by many different accounts of the individual's development. Religious education always will focus upon religious or faith development, but these are not to be seen separately from other kinds of development. Recently Piaget's account of cognitive development and Erikson's portrayal of emotional development have been influential. Let us consider cognitive development for a moment.

Basic to Piaget's account is the definition of cognition as a form of understanding which goes beyond sense experience.[6] Piaget studied the way mental images differ from that which one perceives directly. The internal transformation of a perception is referred to as an "operation." When a child is able to perceive that trees on the horizon are not moving with the automobile in which one is riding, even though they seem to move, that child has performed a cognitive operation on the immediate sense experience. In the same way, the child who knows that the moon is large and far away, rather than small and close at hand, has performed a cognitive operation. Through such operations every child gains a sense of object, self, and causality, to mention only a few of the categories Piaget has studied.

Cognition takes place as a shift from action to operation. In the earliest stage—the sensorimotor stage (birth to two years of age)—the child responds primarily by instinctive actions. By age two, most children can solve simple problems, go around barriers to get what they want, and use verbal sounds to indicate a few basic concepts.

The advent of language presents a whole new set of possibilities for the child and initiates the preoperational stage (ages two to seven). In these years the child gains great facility in the use of language, but there is little sense of constancy of volume, number, time, cause, and so on. The child lives in a world where the immediate impact of experience is overwhelming. Fairy tales and mythical stories are a delight to these children because their minds do not require the consistencies preferred by adults.

By age six, seven, or eight, children are developing a sense of the constancy of object, number, time, and volume in what Piaget calls the state of concrete operations. Children of this age are normally able to apply concepts to particular instances and are capable of calculating, telling time, and writing. Their ideas are often very literal and unyielding, but considerably advanced over the preoperational stage.

The final stage, according to Piaget, is that of formal operations. By this time most young people are able to reason hypothetically about things not present or imaginary, understand the correlation of two or more variables, and in general, think abstractly. With the advent of formal thinking the fullest transformation of sense perceptions has occurred, and a person has the cognitive basis to enter the adult world. Formal thought itself also moves through certain substages, so that the average twelve-year-old is not as mature in cognitive ability as the average twenty-year-old. However, my task here is not to describe the substages, and so I leave the matter at that point.

The relation of cognitive development to faith development has been most carefully explored by Ronald Goldman.[7] His basic thesis is that religious thought requires formal thinking. A child may know something of religious experience before the advent of formal thinking, but the experience always will be less than adequate, from a cognitive point of view. The concept of God, to take the most basic religious concept as our example, is a formal concept. Preoperational and literal (concrete operational) concepts of God are conceptually inadequate and will be seriously revised or cast out by a more mature person. Goldman believes that when children are instructed about religious doctrines prior to the advent of their ability to handle formal concepts, they are inoculated against religion. They later come to believe that what they were taught was false. His conclusion is that we must teach what the child is able to understand—what the child is able to manage cognitively.

In Goldman's view, children of ages five to seven are in a prereligious stage. At that time they move from deifying their parents to parentalizing the deity. A not untypical description of God is this: "God is the man in the moon. He has a round head and he has bent ears. He lives in a round home.''[8] Children of this age receive simply and directly the religion of those who care for them; they are seldom if ever agnostics, but their cognitive understanding is so underdeveloped that Goldman calls it prereligious.

The years from seven to eleven are characterized by Goldman as subreligious. The literal bent of children of this age does not allow them to possess an adequate understanding of basic religious categories. God is usually something of a fairy-tale character, unpredictable, magical, at once loving and angry. Jesus and God are interchangeable. The Bible is to be read magically and literally. There is a dualism between the magical God and natural life. While this is a considerable advance over prereligious thought, a more mature person will cast it out unless it is drastically revised.

Children of twelve and older are normally able to think formally about God. They recognize poetic truth. They are able to consider propositional thought about God and to deliberate about whether they will accept or reject such propositions. They therefore are at a time of deciding whether to accept or reject Christianity. A basic review of Christian teaching is therefore very appropriate by this age. Goldman's description of the influences of cognitive development upon religious development is powerful, but it depends upon what one understands religion to be. We shall return to this point in a moment.

Moral Development

By far the most influential research in moral development during recent years has been done by Lawrence Kohlberg. His work has had, and continues to have, a dramatic impact upon religious education. Kohlberg understands moral judgments to be the result of spontaneous efforts to make sense out of a complex social world.[9] Not surprisingly, this sounds very much like Piaget's description of cognitive thought. Kohlberg further defines moral judgments as normative concepts about human interaction; these concepts are universal, inclusive, consistent, and grounded in objective, impersonal, or ideal grounds.

Kohlberg is of the opinion that the most reliable indicator of moral maturity is moral judgment. The other two candidates, moral conduct and moral emotion, are grossly unreliable. The Hartshorne and May studies of the 1930s concluded that moral behavior is situation specific, and that conclusion has not been overturned since. Similarly, moral emotions such as guilt are poor indicators of either behavior or moral judgment. Kohlberg concludes that moral reasoning can be typed according to its stage of development, even though one cannot predict what specific decisions will be reached by a person of any given stage. Otherwise stated, the maturity of moral reasoning can be typed according to form, though not according to content.

Kohlberg finds three levels of moral development, and two stages at each level. The three levels are named with reference to conformity to convention: preconventional, conventional, and postconventional. At the preconventional level, stage one is oriented to punishment and obedience (ages 3-7). If asked whether or not to "tell on" a playmate, a child of this age is likely to say, "I'd better tell or I'll be spanked." A few years later (ages 8-11) a child is more likely to be in the second stage—naïve instrumental relativism. To the same question, the child is now more likely to answer, "I'll not tell so I will get along better with the others." Stage-two children have a highly developed sense that fairness requires everyone to receive an equal portion, whatever the circumstances. For example, such children have difficulty understanding why older children may stay up later, while they themselves must go to bed.

Once concrete thinking has begun, the conventional level of moral thinking soon follows. Stage three (12-17) is one of interpersonal concordance, wherein a youth is able to understand and take into account the perspectives and intentions of other persons. Justice usually involves conventional images of what is right, including the avoidance of disapproval and of hurting others. Even rebellious youths ordinarily have a group of peers to whom they may turn for support of their moral ideas. The resultant characteristics of moral judgment are the same as for their less rebellious counterparts.

Stage four (ages 18-25) is conventional in another sense. The appeal now is to law and order. Whether one should tell about a friend's misdeed now depends upon whether the deed violates the law or seriously disturbs the public order. Justice is established by the maintenance of the values of one's own society, by doing one's duty. There is as yet no keen sense of the rights of the minority.

The most mature level is postconventional, wherein moral conventions are understood and appreciated, but other considerations are also important. Stage five (age 25 plus) is a matter of social contract. Society becomes an agreement among people of differing convictions, for mutual benefit. Therefore it is in the interest of all that the rights of all individuals, including minorities, be respected. Whether one should tell about the misdeed of a friend will now depend upon the reason the friend acted as he did and consideration of the effects each possible action will have upon the friend and upon the wider communty. Justice therefore is defined in terms of the protection of individual rights.

In stage six (no age given because so few attain this level) one recognizes universal moral principles. Reverence becomes paramount—not for social order, but for the moral principles that are binding upon all societies and all people. Truth-telling is obligatory because it leads to the highest level of human relationship. Justice in a situation consists of the equal consideration of all claims, with all persons being considered as ends and never exclusively as means.

There have been many criticisms of Kohlberg's account of moral development, but they tend to move in the same direction. Kohlberg achieved the power of his analysis by focusing upon the formal conceptual elements and by eliminating the emotive and decisional elements. Many feel that this limits the concept of morality too severely (see

Dykstra and Gilligan); that there are a number of moral virtues besides that of justice (Potter).[10] But Kohlberg's work is so well researched that it cannot possibly be ignored in religious education, which traditionally has included concern for moral education. Interestingly enough, Kohlberg's work has appealed to religious educators of both conservative and liberal theological orientations.

Emotional Development

Without doubt, Sigmund Freud set the framework within which nearly all subsequent discussions of emotional development have taken place in the past century, although very significant alterations have been made in psychoanalytic theory since he first authored it. The revisionist of Freudian theory whose work has had the greatest impact upon religious education is assuredly Erik Erikson. The exclusive focus upon pathology is overcome in Erikson, who has spent much effort describing the "growth crisis of the healthy personality."[11]

Erikson understands a healthy personality, often referred to as ego strength, to be a unity of the personality to the degree that one can actively master the environment and perceive the world and oneself without distortion. The unity of the personality focuses especially upon emotional elements. The healthy personality moves through a series of stages, each characterized by a particular psychosocial attitude. A psychosocial attitude stands between psychological needs and common social perceptions and expectations. The experience of these attitudes is caught by the expression "a sense of"—for example, "a sense of health"; they include one's own conscious *experiences* and feelings, one's way of *behaving* that are observable to others, and deeper *inner states* accessible only to psychological investigation or therapy.[12]

Erikson enumerates eight stages, each characterized by a uniquely different atttude in each person. Nevertheless the attitudes for a given stage are universally the same in that they always stand between two extreme possibilities. In stage one (age 0-1), an infant establishes an attitude somewhere between basic trust and mistrust, depending upon the quality of the relationship with the mother. If the resolution is heavily on the side of mistrust, there is high anxiety, which presages ominously for future stages. On the other hand, even the healthiest trustful attitude will include an element of mistrust, since one cannot be oriented to reality without some degree of mistrust.

Stage two (ages 2-3) is characterized by autonomy versus shame and doubt and is precipitated by the child's increasing ability to exercise self-control, to hold and to let go. The preschool years are completed by stage three (ages 3-6), when the basic attitude is one of initiative versus guilt. Both extremes are the result of the child's ability to use language, anticipate, plan, and carry out activities.

With the school years comes stage four (ages 6-11), accompanied by the attitudinal extremes of industry versus inferiority. The child's ability to master skills such as reading and baseball determines the attitude. The onset of adolescence brings stage five (ages 12-18) with its attitude of identity versus identity confusion. The establishment of an identity attitude is the basis for the adult attitudes.

The first of the adult psychosocial attitudes is found in stage six (ages 19-30). The extremes range from intimacy to isolation; the attitude is precipitated by adult efforts at lasting friendships—for example, the marriage relationship. Middle adulthood (ages 30-65) brings the attitude between generativity and stagnation, which undergirds all those activities that create and carry the culture. The eighth and final stage is one of integrity versus despair, an attitude which results from declining vitalities and the loss of friends through death or other circumstances.

Erikson is like most cognitive theorists in that he attempts to bring together both emotive and cognitive elements. Clearly, he is stronger on the emotive side. Mary Wilcox argues for the inclusion of "emotional, enactive, rational, and imagistic" elements in an approach she calls confluent education.[13] In the same vein, R. S. Peters calls for much more careful attention to the relationship of the rational and the emotive.[14] Every emotion, he contends, has a related concept, even though a mistaken one. The emotion of jealousy presumes that one is being unjustly deprived of what belongs to one.

A recent work by Donald Evans attempts to stand between developmental psychology, religion, and ethics, with the concept of "attitude-virtue."[15] An attitude-virtue has psychological roots, but at the same time it is an ethical and religious orientation. Evans lists attitude-virtues as follows:

> trust and distrust
> humility and pride
> self-acceptance and rejection
> responsibility and irresponsibility
> self-commitment and dissipation
> friendliness and self-preoccupation
> concern and self-indulgence
> contemplation and self-consciousness.

The parallelism with Erikson is more than coincidental. Evans acknowledges that his inspiration came from Erikson, but Evans is attempting a carefully reasoned account of each attitude-virtue, showing how all of them work out in adult life. The significance of Evans' work lies in his effort to provide an ethical and theological account that is clearly rooted in a developmental concept.

Elsewhere, I have argued for protomoral dispositions, established during early childhood and providing the basis for later moral attitudes.[16] During the school years the child develops basic value-attitudes, which in turn are supplemented by belief-attitudes established during adolescence. This leads to experimentation with a way of life during the early adult years. These concepts parallel those of Erikson, Peters, Wilcox, and Evans, but are set in more explicitly ethical terms.

Faith Development

Research on faith development has been much stimulated in the past decade by the original work of James Fowler. Fowler understands faith to be a unity of knowing, doing, and feeling; a qualitative trust that is basic to all human behavior; the core element of the personality.[17] Faith is a person's or a community's "way-of-being-in-relation" to an ultimate environment. This definition of faith indicates that all persons live out of faith, whether they consider themselves to be religious or not, whether they belong to one religious tradition or another. Everyone goes through the stages of faith development, though some may be in religious and some in nonreligious modes.

Prior to age three, by Fowler's account, faith is undifferentiated, while behavior is sensorimotor, and language is still rudimentary. Stage one properly begins about age three, lasts until age seven, and is designated as intuitive-projective. During stage one, a child's behavior is preoperational and episodic. Empathy is rudimentary. Measured by size and power, authority is primarily family oriented. Religious symbols are magical and numinous. The child is "powerfully and permanently influenced by the examples, moods, actions and language of the visible faith of primary adults."[18]

Stage two (ages 7-11) is called mythic-literal. With concrete operational cognitive patterns, the child is capable of narrative drama and simple perspective-taking. Authority is still within the family and those immediately related to it. Instrumental hedonism reigns in the moral realm. Religious symbols are understood in one-dimensional and literal terms. The child takes in the stories, beliefs, and practices of the community to which he or she belongs.

Stage three persons (ages 12-18) possess a synthetic-conventional faith. With the early capacity for formal thought, youth can use symbols, though often without being explicit about the meaning. Religious symbols are multidimensional, but often conventional and oriented to the authority of tradition. Ability at multiple role-taking makes complex drama possible. Individuals usually reflect the class norms to which they belong. Morality is first a matter of interpersonal concord, but may progress to the stage of law and order. Youth often has a wide range of social involvements, and faith offers help in providing a "meaningful synthesis" within the complexities of life.

Stage four (18-30) is called individuative-reflexive by Fowler. Formal thought processes should be well established, with the growing ability to be explicit about the concepts one is using. Authority has become more pragmatic or ideological, and the social class norms are self-chosen. Morality tends to be law-and-order oriented, coupled with a reflective relativism and a criticism of ideas. Stage four persons take responsibility for their commitments. They recognize and try to deal with these polar tensions: individuality versus community, subjectivity versus objectivity, self-fulfillment versus service to others, the relative versus the absolute.

Stage five (ages 30-40) faith is conjunctive. Formal thought has become dialectical, with an interplay between symbolic and conceptual meaning. People understand the mutuality between their community and other communities, and they understand the dialectic of multiple belief-patterns. They are able to transcend social-class norms with a reflective relativism and possess a drive to find a unity of symbolic, conceptual, and other belief elements. They are able to affirm their own truth without denying that of others and are willing to take the risk of living toward the coming of a more nearly universal community.

Stage six (age 40 plus) is simply called universalizing. Formal thinking is able to go beyond dialectics to synthesis, which means that there is both symbolic coherence and close touch with actual experience. There is a sense of the interrelatedness of all reality. Authority rests more upon "what is" than upon any person or group. One goes beyond class norms to universally human norms; hence morality is both universal and critical. There is a willingness to relate without pretense to all persons, no matter what their age or stage of development. Religious symbols have the power to point to the wider inclusive reality in which we all live, referred to by Christians as the kingdom of God.

The reader will quickly see from this description that Fowler attempts to bring together cognitive, moral, emotional, and other elements in his description of faith development. Unlike Erikson, Fowler does not insist that persons inevitably move from one stage to another. A person may live his or her life in a stage-three faith. Because of the newness of Fowler's work, it may yet make its greatest impact upon religious education in the future.

The Learner

Having reviewed the cognitive, moral, emotional, and faith dimensions of development, let us now consider the whole person as a learner. A developmental view puts certain constraints upon learning theory. The two clearest types of learning theory are the behaviorist and the Gestalt. We may be able to account for the content of a particular stage by a behaviorist theory, but we cannot account for the movement from one stage to another. To be sure, we may be able to account for a child's view that God is the moon by the simple association of the child's seeing the moon and being asked the question. Yet we must go beyond behaviorism to account for this child's abandonment of the moon-god for a Heavenly Parent. The movement from one stage to another requires more than a theory of association of stimulus and responses.

Gestalt learning theory can be coordinated with the concept of development if one considers each stage as a differing and maturing ability to perceive various relationships and patterns. The four-year-old child sees only patterns of immediate sense experience, such as the power of larger persons, while the twelve-year-old can see formal conceptual patterns, such as the idea of love.

In the same way, an existentialist or hermeneutic view of learning must be modified to fit the concept of development. Existentialism features the disclosure or discovery of meaning, while hermeneutics indicates the different levels at which meaning may be understood. According to a developmental view there are limits on what a person will discover or understand, set by the stages within which a person is located. At the same time there is an infinite variety of disclosures possible in any given stage. One of the fathers of existentialism, Søren Kierkegaard, suggested that all persons tend to pass through four stages: aesthetic, moral, universal religious, and particular religious. There are lines of analogy to Kohlberg's preconventional, conventional, and postconventional levels. Clearly, an existentialist learning theory may be coordinated with the concept of development.

Let me suggest that learning always involves four very deep-seated processes which engage the whole person. There are basic personality processes, or if you like, ego processes. Learning, to begin, involves awareness. To experience directly, to possess activities and words for that experience, increases awareness and, as a result, learning. The fact that after a painful accident a person is unable to remember what happened does not topple my claim. The learning (fear of autos, let us say) occurred at the moment of the now-forgotten accident. Relearning the attitude toward autos probably will require that the person recover some awareness of the event, perhaps under hypnosis.

A second process is that of intentionality. Profound learning requires the interest and intention of the learner. As long as one ignores or resists, little of the intended learning will take place; awareness therefore will include awareness only of what one wants to learn and how one intends to go about it. Even though the attention span of young children is short, the principles of attention and intention still rule.

Coherence is the third learning process. Instinctively, the ego works at finding coherence among disparate experiences. This can be done simply by stringing them together in a story, or it can be done more conceptually by giving an explanation. In any case, each person is continually engaged in finding lines and patterns of coherence, imaginal connectedness, and cognitive relationships in the multilayered and multifaceted experience of living. Any contribution to the process of finding coherence through activity, feeling, imaginative symbol, or concept will aid the person's learning.

The fourth and last of the personal learning processes is that of mutuality. Every person is engaged in interaction with various groups. The significant groups are those in which the ruling patterns heavily influence what a person learns. The ability to help establish a community with norms that are fair, open, considerate of individual difference, inquiring, and filled with enthusiasm will have an effect upon each person in that group.

The processes of learning criss-cross the four modes of learning: the active, the emotional, the intuitive, and the rational. Activity is instinctive with the organism and its perceptual capacities. The earliest instinctive activities of infancy are replaced by the involved and considered activities of adulthood. Piaget suggests that all cognition is covert activity. Until an infant can picture in the mind what he or she will do next, there is no possibility of language and no possibility of conceptual thought. This suggests that activity is more than an accompaniment to learning—it is the beginning and basis of all learning. In John Dewey's famous summary expression, We learn by doing. The statement would be much more true to Dewey if it were phrased, We learn by the interaction of behavior and concept. In this form the importance of giving verbal expression to what one is learning becomes more clear.

A second method of learning is the emotional. In the emotivist view, activity is a covert emotion. Educators of the emotions consider it axiomatic that one learns to give verbal expression to emotions. When one says that one feels miserable and aggressive, it brings some limit to a feeling that might otherwise be acted out in harmful ways. Similarly, the expression of joy in a group celebration enlarges and fulfills that feeling.

A third mode of learning is the rational, logical, and verbal. In Piaget's account, cognition involves a transformation of perceptions, as I have described. Such transformations are the foundation of logical concepts. The ability to use language and to think conceptually are linked, and learning is not complete with either perception or action alone. Full learning occurs as experience is cognitively transformed. Learning, then, always will involve either implicit or explicit concepts. Action and experience must be accompanied by verbal expression about what is being learned.

The fourth mode is the intuitive, imaginative, and metaphoric. In imaginative thinking the forms of thought flow without strict attention to logical relationships. The ability to intuit and to imagine is the basis for all thinking; thus the cultivation of intuition can deepen thinking. Stories, literature, and poetry exercise the metaphoric and imaginative abilities.

The processes and modes I have just described are present in every normal person at all times during consciousness. A person is either shaping or being shaped by the environment, and learning is a dynamic balance between the two. The learner therefore invents what is learned. Seemingly ancient truths must be reinvented by each learner. This balance of shaping and being shaped between the learner and what is learned makes clear how deeply self-engaging learning is.

I cannot conclude this discussion without mentioning certain principles of learning that have been experimentally established:

    a. the principle of readiness
    b. the principle of conflict and resolution
    c. the principle of multiple perspectives
    d. the principle of environmental level

According to the principle of readiness, persons learn only at their current stages. A person in the stage of concrete thinking cannot possibly understand a formal explanation, nor will attention be given to identity questions until the competency attitude has been established. Studies of moral reasoning suggest that a person can understand the moral explanation no more than one stage beyond his or her present stage; therefore the best chance of learning exists when the person is challenged by a level of development only slightly beyond his or her current stage.

The principle of conflict and resolution is based upon the theoretical assumption that learning occurs as the learner attempts to bring coherence to disparate experiences. Arguments and disagreements among peers often stimulate the cognitive growth of group members. In the same manner, emotional conflicts may stimulate emotional growth. In both cases, the ability to identify and give verbal expression to the resolution of the conflict is important to learning.

The principle of multiple perspectives is derived from research showing that persons learn by having different roles in a variety of experiences. The comprehension of the various roles in a situation is basic to moral development, and also to emotional, cognitive, and faith development. As learning activities and games expand role experiences, stages of development are likely to increase in many dimensions.

Finally, the principle of environmental level suggests that a person learns when the environment contains a level of stimulation slightly beyond his or her own. Peers stimulate one another to learn, and slightly more advanced peers stimulate those not quite so advanced. The obverse is also true—a person is less likely to learn when the environment contains no such stimulation.

I have pictured the learner as one who is always attempting to consolidate what already has been learned as well as to include newer challenges. Learning is healthy when there is a balance between the two. Defensive action may occur either as a resistance to change or as a groping for change—a groping that is never consolidated around the inner core of belief. This openness to the balance between consolidation and reintegration is the way to maturity.

The Goal

The goal of Christian education, from a developmental point of vew, is the maturity of persons—that persons become more aware of themselves, their communities, and their world; more intentional in making choices and in relating to others. Maturity means risking the discovery of wider and deeper levels of meaning and becoming more interactive and responsive to other persons. In a word, maturity means being open to the next stage of development in the various dimensions of life. The goal of education will be achieved when each person is challenged to respond at his or her own stage of readiness. This view sees education as taking place with responsive and responsible persons, within a world community of responsive and responsible persons.[19]

The developmental approach to Christian education purposes that every person receive and respond to the grace of God in Jesus Christ; that all persons be joined together in an inclusive community, with the Spirit of mutual respect and love—in the words of Ephesians 4:13, that we might be "measured by nothing less than the full stature of Christ." A mature Christian is ever more aware of God's love, ever more intentional about God's will, ever more respectful of God's providence, and ever more responsive to God's community. The goal of Christian education, then, is to provide an environment that stimulates each person, at whatever his or her stage of faith development.

Let us consider whether the goal of education is that a person be equally well developed in all respects. Clearly, not everyone can be. The encouragement of the cognitive, or the emotional, or the moral stage of development is entirely appropriate as long as the other stages are not entirely ignored. The Bible acknowledges that some people have a greater gift for faith than others. The various gifts of the Spirit would seem to result from the relationship between faith and the other developmental levels. Surely this is true within the developmental framework of the book of Ephesians.

The Teacher

The concept of development allows for a variety of teaching styles: more instructional or more process-oriented, more directive or less directive, more or less formal. It would be a mistake to suggest that the developmental point of view requires one particular way to teach.

The concept does, however, point to some definitive or essential characteristics of the teacher. All teachers must have some qualities of guide, sponsor, challenger, observer, manager, and diagnostician. We will recall that learning comes from interaction and challenge, in which the learner seeks a new pattern of coherence. The teacher may challenge by a variety of means, but more probably will help shape experiences in which the learner will be challenged at an appropriate level. Much learning goes on between peers who share the same experiences.

The principle of readiness requires that the teacher be a careful and patient observer of the learner, so as to become clear about the learner's stage of development. The teacher also must manage and arrange materials so that they are available and challenging to learners at different stages of development.

The principle of conflict and resolution requires that the teacher be able to help a learner identify points of conflict or express emotional conflict. The teacher must also encourage the student in efforts to express resolution to conflict. Conflict may take the form of argument with a problem, a reading, a personal experience, or a challenge by another student. The teacher knows the importance of such conflict, as long as the support necessary for resolution is present.

The principle of multiple perspectives suggests that a teacher provide many different types of interaction and many different role opportunities. Various activities—readings, games, drama—will add to the depth of learning. Teaching means encouraging action, interaction, and coherent verbal expression, in proper relation to one another.

The principle of environmental level suggests an atmosphere with both assurance and challenge. The physical environment, the schedule of activities, and the atmosphere of the group should be both supportive and challenging. There should be fair responses to each learner at his or her own level; emotional support and conflict should be acknowledged and responded to at the appropriate level; intellectual challenge should be at a level the learner can understand; and faith assurance and challenge should be given at the level of the learner's faith development. An environment that challenges learners in these ways should be one in which much learning is fostered.

The teacher in religious education must be as sensitive as any other teacher about the readiness of each learner. Since faith is as much a matter of conflict and resolution as is other learning, receiving and guiding conflict is basic to faith development. Religious education that attempts to eliminate all conflict is also likely to eliminate any profound learning about faith. The mixture of activity and verbal expression is basic in Christian education. The teacher of religious education should provide an atmosphere of environmental challenge, fairness, acceptance, support, and a level of faith development that meets the developmental stage of the learners.

To some extent, developmental teaching must be individualized. Whether or not activities are in a group, the teacher must be in touch with the progress of development in each individual. The teaching must also be self-engaging. Activites may take place at an everyday humdrum level, at a more symbolic level, or even more deeply at a self-engaging level, where the learner is inventing the material and being changed (invented) in the process. The teacher may need to go through days of humdrum activity to reach occasions of self-engaging learning.

In a word, the teacher has a vision of what the learner can become. The teacher's confidence and challenge become an element in the synthesis which make up the next stage of development. In this sense the teacher is a sponsor. It seems axiomatic that only a teacher who is open to the next stage of development for himself or herself can be sensitive to that openness in the learner. So the teacher must have the qualities of guide, sponsor, challenger, observer, manager, diagnostician, and model. A teacher might manage without some of these qualities, but without any of them, the person might as well give up teaching.

Setting and Content

The concept of development has no particular setting that leads to high-intensity learning. A whole variety of settings is possible. What would seem to be critical is that the setting provide: (1) some interaction; and (2) some stimulation of a type appropriate to the readiness of the learner. Besides these minimal characteristics, the setting ideally would include the following characteristics: (3) interactions with peers as well as with teacher; (4) space and equipment for a variety of activities, both physical and verbal; and (5) a functioning community that exercises the skills to be learned.

Since developmental learning occurs in much wider ways than does formal education, much of the research on developmental learning has been done in informal settings. Piaget carried out many of his observations in his own family and on the playground in the school. The descriptions of learning that fit the developmental concept may easily occur in such informal settings as family, play group, church picnic, or hike. The informal setting may be a larger intergenerational setting, a smaller peer group, or individual play, meditation, or work. Piaget, Kohlberg, Fowler, and Wilcox all have frequently used one-to-one interviews. The one-to-one relationship is critical in the concept of development, since without it, the teacher can scarcely know a learner's stage of development.

Formal settings such as a small group, a class group, or a school also may be organized around the concept of development, as indeed many are. Such settings require the possibility of attention to individuals, opportunity for a wide variety of interaction and behavioral expression, and an environment stimulating to the developmental stage of the learners.

Religious education therefore may rely upon both formal and informal settings within a developmental concept. Church activities featuring family activities, picnics, and other informal gatherings may be chosen to meet the developmental needs of the persons attending. The church school, then, would be a vehicle for focusing more directly upon the particular stage of development of each person. The school should allow the designing of experiences that challenge each person in the appropriate way. Unfortunately, some schools become so routine-oriented that they actually lose touch with the development of the learners and as a result, cease to function as schools.

When one turns to content, the concept of development has fewer implications for what is learned than for how it should be processed. Content should be selected to allow for readiness (graded), individualized, evocative at the appropriate level, full of variety, and inclusive of active, feeling, and moral, as well as cognitive illustrations. It is critical to individualize the content to meet the learners at the point of readiness. Therefore content should be examined to judge whether the concepts are at the right level, whether the emotional appeal is appropriate, whether the assumptions about moral development are fitting, and whether there are opportunities to become self-engaging.

Stories have been widely used by Piaget and Kohlberg. Play and ritual are emphasized by Erikson. Dilemmas and problem-solving questions are favorites of several researchers. Extended one-to-one interviewing is another popular approach. Drama, simulation, and many types of planning activities, with various people playing out various roles, have been recommended. Goldman emphasizes that the content must be related to the life themes of the learners. Wilcox suggests value-clarification activities. All these types of content are quite appropriate in religious education.

Limits of Development

Having examined the concept of development and its implications for religious education, I will conclude by asking, What are the limits of the concept? The attempt to find a universal temporal ground plan for human life is intriguing, but the question always remains: Is not the very concept relative to our culture and historical epoch? Kohlberg has researched his developmental sequence in other cultures in order to demonstrate its universality, and his data are impressively supportive of his view. They offer evidence that more mature persons are to be found in the United States than in some other cultures, which again raises the question: Are we defining maturity from an American point of view? In religious education, does Fowler's account of stage-six faith unduly reflect his own Methodist orientation?

A related question has to do with the sequence of the stages. Is it actually invariable as assumed? Could a child not perceive his or her own self-interest *before* being punishment-oriented? My own view is that the protomoral dispositions of trust, autonomy, and initiative are more basic to moral development than is orientation to punishment, and therefore a kind of self-interest is equally original to the orientation to punishment. This objection does not challenge the concept of development itself, but rather the presumed description of development. In religious education, does faith develop in a given sequence, or are the patterns diverse and multifarious? Since there are good biblical and theological grounds for the belief that faith moves from lesser to greater maturity, the concept of development in regard to Christian faith cannot be dismissed out of hand.

Also, may a person not regress or backslide, after having achieved a particular stage? Psychoanalytic thought speaks of regression, something cognitive theory avoids. But ego-analytic theory assumes that regression is "in the service of the ego" at its current stages of development: The regression is to consolidate the stage toward which the person is now progressing and is not an actual moving backward against the developmental pattern. Kohlberg has a similar explanation for youth as it moves from a law-and-order orientation, through a period of hedonistic relativism, to a conception of social contract. The relativism seems to be that of an earlier period, but he sees it as a passing phase, serving to move it to the next stage.

In religious education, some persons not infrequently come to repudiate religious faith. A developmental framework would consider the possibility that this is a passing phase in service of greater faith. Please remember that, as defined, all human beings are at some level of faith. Biblically, a backslider is far more difficult to reach than one who never has been a Christian. Developmentally considered, a backslider is more likely to consolidate his or her reaction to religion at a higher level of faith than is an unbeliever. We may conclude that it is unlikely that persons simply move backward against their development.

Another very similar question: Do persons move through all, or simply some of the stages? In Erikson's model, persons move through all the stages, though the level depends a great deal on what has been achieved in previous stages. In the cognitive model, especially in moral and faith development, a person may be arrested at any particular stage. This is simply a difference in the models, which needs further clarification.

Also frequently asked: May a person not learn an attitude (Erikson) or a "schema" (Piaget) after the stage has passed where it was to be learned? The answer is that he or she may revisit and revise an attitude or schema of an earlier period, but of course this is done within the framework of the present stage of development.

Still another question: Does not the concept of development stand in opposition to the idea of conversion? Clearly, the concept of development stands against the idea that the only kind of conversion is the momentary, once-and-for-all kind. While this may be the case for some—even for many—for others, conversion will come as a series of lesser conversions. And there may be those happy souls who always have known themselves to be Christians. The concept of development, as we have been describing it, contains the ideas of crisis, reorientation, and fundamental change, as well as continuity. Each stage involves a crisis and a resolution. The years of youth have a special crisis of orientation—the identity crisis. But the twenties have their crisis of community; and the mid-years, their crisis of generativity. Each presents an element of conversion. At the same time, a person may shift loyalty away from secular symbols and commitments, to Christian symbols. Such a total reorientation is a dramatic conversion, but one that does not contradict the concept of faith development. Faith development is contradicted if conversion is so defined that it includes only a one-time dramatic reorientation.

This is perhaps the most fundamental question: Does not the universality implied in the concept of development contradict the concept of history? The first answer is that development may be justified simply on the pragmatic ground that it is useful. If it is productive of intended learning and if it gives the teacher a model for relating to the learners, then the question of universality may be irrelevant.

Let me pause for a moment to point out that the concept of development does not necessarily include the idea of inevitable moral betterment. It does imply increasingly complex interaction, in preestablished pattern and sequence, with what has gone before and with what is coming. To the extent that a person must move through the stages (Erikson), there may be moral gain or decline at any stage. Although the moral gain from previous stages is maintained in successive stages, continuing moral gain is not inevitable. Since a person need not move through all stages (Fowler), a person who is resting on a given stage will not inevitably progress. The idea of inevitable moral progress therefore is not implicit in the idea of development as it is being used here.

But to return to the question of history. For our purposes, we need simply point out that the twentieth century has largely given up the notion that history develops; certainly the idea of moral progress in history is in serious question. The idea of a ground plan with an invariant sequence simply does not fit history as we understand it.

To the extent that individuals are historical beings, do they not transcend the concept of development? I believe that the answer to this question is yes. The developmental character of personality is rooted in the organic structure of life. But personality is also shaped by its participation in the process of history. To that degree, individuals and groups transcend developmental categories, but not absolutely. Cultural and historical participation always is limited by the developmental stage in which a person is to be found.

Conclusion

We have examined the concept of development and found these elements: ground plan, invariable sequence, increasing complexity, interaction, and goal. Then we looked at the way the idea of development is used in Christian education. In cognitive development, Ronald Goldman describes prereligious, subreligious, and religious stages. In moral development, Lawrence Kohlberg describes preconventional, conventional, and postconventional stages. In emotional development, I discussed the development of religious, ethical, and psychosocial attitudes. James Fowler has described six stages of faith development.

We then turned to a discussion of the learner, the teacher, the goal, the settings, and the content of religious education, from the point of view of development. We concluded that though the concept has many theoretical problems, it is still very useful. Aside from the need for continuing research, the developmental approach is limited by the concept of history, which in our epoch is not considered to contain all the elements of development.

Religious education in the twentieth century has attempted to build a church school system around the idea of religious development, and current research suggests that the idea has continuing potential. There are many areas in which that research could be expanded. The idea of religious development remains a powerful and faithful way to build a religious educational program. When one sees its similarity to ancient thought, one is persuaded that it will continue to be powerful for centuries to come.

5

Liberation and the Future of Christian Education
Allen J. Moore

A true liberation education in the churches of North America must begin with the critical awareness that we are part of the world problem and that our experience is totally different from that of the oppressed people with whom this approach was generated. Allen Moore warns us of our natural tendency to co-opt liberation language, to personalize its agenda, and therefore to trivialize its power for social transformation. He proposes that Christian education become prophetic education, to challenge oppressive social structures from the perspective of Christian eschatology. Such a form of Christian education will, in fact, challenge many of the church's own programs and techniques of education, as well as the liaison between church education and public schooling. Prophetic Christian education will be concerned with the development of a new Christian consciousness which will be aware of the global context of oppression and will lead Christians in constructing new, faithful, life-styles.

There is a note of irony in North American religious leaders' present preoccupation with the subject of liberation. Even the least among us is not politically oppressed, and the abundance we take for granted transforms our understanding of the realities of poverty into a figment of our imagination. We are undoubtedly motivated in part by our guilt for having so much and in part by our partial awareness that the institutions we represent have contributed directly, as well as indirectly, to the oppression experienced so intensely by the people of the Third World. The churches, with their extensive commitments of economic and human resources to the maintenance of institutional life, stand also as reminders that the Christian response has been totally inadequate toward that majority of the global people who live in intense want. The very subject of this paper again raises the classical conflict between the nurturing ministry of the church and the church's mission and sacrificial service to the world.

The thesis of this paper is that Christian education must recover its historical relationship to Christian social action. It is this legacy of the religious education movement that liberation is pushing the churches to preserve, in spite of the current pressures to withdraw from the world and to turn inward again to an individualistic and spiritualized form of education.

There is irony also in our present preoccupation with the future. It might be well for us to take an inventory, counting the many conferences we attend or books we read that have to do with future matters. What is it about the future that so deeply captures our attention? Possibly it is our own insecurity about where the present may be taking us.

Social commentators suggest that for the first time within the North American experience, we no longer can look forward to a life of better *things*.[1] The unlimited future we have taken for granted has now become limited. We have come to accept our way of life as a normative standard, and this has left us both self-righteous and insensitive to the plight of others. The combination of American pragmatism, with its emphasis on "things working out," and religious pietism, with its theme of a better life in the "sweet by and by," has blinded us to the harsh realities of a social history that now confronts us and demands a response.

There is much self-interest in our concern for the future. We are not only looking desperately for some clue to the survival of the church as an institution but also for some assurance that our personal futures will be good to us. Note, for example, how often professional issues such as status, finances, and recognition come up for discussion.

And yet today, particular futures are intimately tied to the universal future of the whole of humankind. We can no longer be concerned about one segment of society and ignore another with a future that may be more urgent.[2] This is true of Christian education, particularly when viewed from a liberation perspective. The issue of the future of Christian education is related to the question of the resolution of the struggle for human freedom. What is somewhat disconcerting is to know that *we* are a part of the human problem of oppression and that it has become problematic whether we can be a part of the solution.

Unwittingly, we have adopted the ideology of survival, with its concern for the preservation of the established order and the middle-center as a way of life. Let us examine both the people served by Christian education and the ethos that supports the church and the other institutions of middle-class society. It is difficult, if not impossible, for us to understand and identify with Marxist-oriented movements calling for the end of the present social structure and the creation of a radical new order. This is why the progressive view of the future held by First-World people and the dialectic *(opposites in conflict)* view found among the Third-World liberationists seem beyond reconciliation. Although it is not necessary at this point for Christian educators to accept a Marxist view of history, we would do well to give more attention to a Christian view of history. Our belief in eschatology (I assume there is a modest belief, at least) suggests that history always holds forth the promise that there will be an end to things as they now are. This implies an approach to Christian education based not on survival and preservation, but on possibilities in the future which the present has not yet disclosed. If we are to be open to learnings that can be gleaned from the liberation movements, we must begin by recognizing that a basic change in attitude and approach to our world is the first requirement.

I

Any attempt to renew Christian education by appropriating the liberation idea runs the risk of trivializing the concept.

The liberation movements in theology and education have emerged primarily in the Latin American context, where oppression and poverty are historical realities, not ideas to be examined and debated. One problem of North American Christian educators, when we talk about liberation, is that our cultural experience is extremely foreign to the experience of the peasants who gave rise to a need for liberation. Paulo Freire recognized this and cautioned that in the First World, liberation either would become another technique for education or it would be idealized as an optional life-style.[3]

Freire's pedagogical methods were worked out in Latin America with persons who were both illiterate and disfranchised politically. His imagination as an educator and his understanding of the psychology of the peasants are demonstrated in his educational praxis. Persons learned how to read, not with the usual primary readers designed to build vocabulary, but through political action, using the documents that were essential to their political welfare.

Similarly, Freire used photographs of the daily life of the peasants as a way to sharpen their perception about what was going on around them and to stimulate what he called generative themes—powerful symbols of the contradictions in their lives.

These rather inductive forms of education can be readily appropriated into the progressive and experiential patterns of education found in most liberal Protestant churches. This is possible especially in the present religious education climate, where there is a preoccupation with educational techniques. But as Freire suggests, apart from the cultural context in which they were formulated, these methods would serve only to reinforce a consciousness that is subjective and personal and would not lead to political revolution. Political action is possible only within a context in which radical change is not merely an option but is urgently necessary for human freedom.

Furthermore, Freire cautions against the idealization of liberation, either by abstracting the concept as a subject of discussion (e.g., a course *about* liberation, rather than engaging in liberating acts) or in compelling all education to become liberation education. One needs only observe the extent to which North Americans are free to "play at reformer" to realize how great this temptation is. Poverty can become just another life-style in an affluent society where persons can afford to reject their material possessions, knowing it is not a permanent condition.[4]

There is possibly nothing more empty today than the works of the social reformer or the good deeds of the well-intentioned Christian. It is this desire to do something for someone else or to solve the problems of others that has been the characteristic response of liberal Christian education. We look on at a distance (a Sunday morning discussion group) and make decisions about what will make life better for someone else.

The irrelevancy of the social reformer today is illustrated by the play *Born in the Gardens* by English writer Peter Nichols. It is the story of a Labor-party member who appears regularly on television on behalf of the starving people of the world, but who comes close to the problems only when he looks at the pictures collected by his staff to illustrate the reports. In the meanwhile, away from Parliament, this social reformer eagerly seeks the good life of a gentleman, enjoys the benefits of a mistress, and is preoccupied with buying every new technical gadget for his home.

As Christians, we are motivated by our view of charity to help the unfortunate people of the world to a better way of life. We do this both by trying to identify with them and through programs of social service and other forms of charitable acts. In this way we can reach out to persons in need without making a far-reaching change in our own position in society. We can also maintain an emotional and spatial distance which serves to limit our real involvement in human suffering.

For most of us, the goal is the *reform* of the established social structures. Seldom do we within the North American scene envision the *total destruction* of the social system for the sake of political freedom and the economic survival of others. For Freire, the humanization of life requires radical *new* political structures; for us, it means new psychological structures and some basic, but not radical, changes in our society.

It is commonly recognized that reformers in this country operate with a minimum risk to their individualism and to their social positions. The young radicals of the 1960s enjoyed financial and social support from their families and from other institutions of the established society, including the church. Although their actions were controversial and even caused some political reprisals, they were to a great extent acting according to the traditions of a democratic society. What is most interesting is that almost all these young radicals have found themselves back in their former social position and within the establishment they sought to reform. It is this kind of stylization of revolution that Freire has called upon the North American churches not to promote. Advocating liberation education is not the same as being a part-time social "reformer" or forming fashionable educational programs. Liberation means escape from a system where someone *does something for you*. The fundamental idea is that *you learn to help yourself*.

Liberation education has its grounding in a dialectic ideology that reflects the actual experience of people who have never known any way of life but oppression and for whom social revolution becomes the *only way* out of their hopeless situation. Few of us can comprehend the true nature of total oppression, much less identify with it. Oppression for us is the inability to do what pleases us or to get our way on a social issue. Today among young adults, it is fashionable to adopt the life-style of nonaffluence because of psychological dissatisfaction with their relationship to the majority of society or for other personal reasons. This is not to imply that there are not deep social injustices within the North American context and that there are not a host of persons who are being robbed of their humanity by an inequitable social system. What is being said here is that for affluent and politically franchised individuals, the idea of liberation may become more fashionable than a radical reexamination of political and economic structures. Adopting a life-style represented by old clothes (prewashed jeans are now sold to this crowd), or becoming a social dropout because of the inability to cope with the structures of authority, is a long way from being an oppressed peasant in Latin America. In fact, it is the very fact of our affluence that allows us to *choose* alternative styles for living—a choice that just is not available to the oppressed. To turn their situation into a new social fashion for Christian education can serve only to distort their real plight. I do not wish to depreciate the sincerity of our new social activists or criticize the good that may come from their efforts. It is the "role playing" that needs critical examination, and the function of Christian education is to help persons find a social witness consistent with their social context and to do more than act out the plight of other people whom we do not know and whose life we cannot experience.

Juan Luis Segundo has written more directly on this issue of "cheap revolution." He points out that the adoption of the "terminology of liberation" by the churches has served only to water down its content and empty it of any significant meaning. It is possible, as Segundo has suggested, to mouth the words while at the same time going on as before.[5] Christian education's adaptation of the language and methods of liberation runs the risk of fostering an inauthentic life-style, leading the churches to believe falsely that they are on the side of the oppressed.

Our beginning point is with a *critical* awareness of the experiences of injustice within the North American scene—including within the church itself. The substitution of the experiences of another time and place only serves as a stumbling block to the freedom and self-determination of those who really are oppressed. As Segundo argues, a theology of liberation begins not with oppression *out there* somewhere, but with the new and decisive questions which arise out of the present reality (social context) in which *we find ourselves.*[6] Only when "profound and enriching questions are asked about a real situation" can the gospel be appropriated for that situation, and a new ministry (such as education) be formed. We cannot just appropriate the agenda of another people.[7] This means, of course, that our task is to perceive "critically" our role in the global oppression that permits the majority of the world's people to live in poverty, unliberated.

In our scene, the gospel is still understood by the ordinary participant in Christian education in individualistic terminology (e.g., "the church should concern itself with spirituality, not social issues"). The Bible continues to be read against the social background of economic capitalism (e.g., the accumulation of wealth is a "blessing"). Our task involves more than calling persons to the social aspects of the gospel. It involves helping them locate themselves in the injustices of the world with new awareness and form a new Christian consciousness for themselves. Both these learnings come not from being *told* ("taught"), but by being enabled to become directly involved in what is going on in the world. More particularly, the social situation in which Christian education is now taking place includes a commitment to expansion and growth at all cost, the abuse of economic and military power, and the rape of the environment through uncontrolled technology. There is, in addition, a lack of real commitment to address the many forms of human injustice and discrimination, especially the subtle forms of racism and sexism.[8] The point is that "critical reflection on praxis" begins with a new awareness of our context and the real history that is taking place.

What is suggested here is that we avoid turning to liberation literature in the hope that we will find a new design to benefit Christian education and help the churches survive in the future. Instead, the message of liberation demands our active participation in the struggle for humanizing life. This requires a critical awareness of our role in the oppression of brothers and sisters in other places and the human injustices that are at the doorstep of the church. The result may prove to be fewer programs of Christian education and more changes in our personal life-styles and in the way the church forms its institutional life.

II

When viewed from the perspective of liberation, life-style becomes a basic issue to be addressed by Christian education. Until recently, life-style has had the connotation of becoming free to be who one wants to be. It referred to personal identity ("I am") becoming manifest in the way one chose to live ("doing my thing"). The educational task was to promote consistency between the internal awareness of self and the external presentation of that self in daily life, or what Erikson called the "continuity of the I."

Life-style also has a moral or value dimension. The way one lives expresses what one really values. Moral education therefore requires more than admonition—it requires opportunities to reflect upon the way one actually lives and what one's choices say about morality. This suggests that Christian education in the future certainly will need to give greater attention to helping persons come to a new consciousness of the values that are professed, versus those that are chosen in the everyday experience of living. Almost without exception, persons are inconsistent as Christians in what they say they believe and in what they represent by the way they live. Don Browning has given attention to this issue by advising that the church give more attention to practical everyday life.[9] In fact, many people who profess to be Christian actually choose values in practice that are secular and self-serving.

Life-style might be defined as a pattern of beliefs, values, and attitudes which can be described and characterized, and which are manifested in the way a person chooses to live.[10] There is also a personal dimension, in that life-style describes the unique and existential meanings that find expression in all the actions and behaviors that make up a personal way of life. It is the way one faces or approaches the world, as well as the value assumptions reflected in the various activities of one's life.

Life-style at the same time encompasses a larger phenomenon than the idosyncrasies of a single individual. The preoccupation of Christian education with *the* individual has led to a neglect of those social or collective values and behaviors that become the shared way of life for a group of persons. Even among Roman Catholics, formation is directed more toward the spiritual growth of the individual than toward the development of a total group of people who have a common or shared approach to the world.

It was Max Weber who introduced the concept into sociological literature by defining life-style as a subculture of people formed around a shared way of life, based upon commonly held values and commitments. Life-style, then, can be understood as a way of describing the *ethos*, or spirit, which marks the distinctive way a people live in the larger society. It is that which *distinguishes* a group and gives it recognition and acknowledgment. In my own tradition, the "Methodist people" stood out in the larger culture because of their commitment to a methodological way of life and their exuberant spirit.

This may be close to the idea of "conscientization" in Freire's works.[11] Conscientization is both an individual experience and the shared experience of a people who are acting together in history. A way of life is not determined from thinking *about* the world but is formed from the shared praxis (human "action-reflection on the world, on reality"). It is in this critical approach to the world that basic attitudes, values, and beliefs are formed and people are humanized or liberated. Conscientization is a life lived within the consciousness of history ("insertion in history"), "denouncing" and "transforming" this history in order that freedom can be shared by those who have no freedom. Freire writes,

> There is no conscientization without historical commitment . . . historical awareness. It is a critical insertion into history. It means that men take on a role as subjects making the world, remaking the world; it asks men to fashion their existence out of the material that life offers them.[12]

This raises an interesting issue for Christian educators.

How can the churches form a Christian people who are "in the world but not of the world"? How can the church itself be liberated as an institution in order to actively participate in the transformation of history rather than being caught like a pawn in the changing fashions of time?

There is certainly need for a more critical awareness of the meanings represented in the way the people we teach approach the world. Such criticalness will not arise from discussions about morality, but from reflection on moral actions (life-style) by the people who call themselves Christian and who gather weekly under that vision.

Segundo puts the issue much more strongly. He believes that the church's pastoral action (which would include education) should lead to a clarification of commitment and to the identification of those who are willing to share in the Christian praxis. The majority in the church, according to Segundo, are cultural Christians and do not share a *true* Christian conscience.[13] Christian education cannot, therefore, be neutral. It must serve to help persons be critical of their commitments and to *separate* those who are seeking a new awareness of the gospel for the world's oppressed from those who are Christians for the convenience of belonging to the social elite.

In a less radical way, the traditional nurturing work of Christian education can serve to help persons become more critical of the way they live in the daily routines of the world, discriminating between more authentic expressions of Christian commitment and the social fashions of our day. The liberation movements may be pushing North American Christians to draw the meaning of the Christian way of life more closely and to reinvent the kind of church *ethos* that once characterized the Methodists, the Calvinists, the Mennonites, the Brethren, and others. As cultural Christians, it has become easier for us to be "of the world" and to choose secularized values that make for social respectability, than to stand over against the world. Segundo's criticism is that present so-called religious values are relegated largely to the private and personal side of life. The church functions in established society primarily as a promoter of social harmony, and its basic gestures in the world serve the welfare of the privileged rather than of the oppressed. This is not to suggest that there are no prophetic gestures by the church, but these come largely from the edges of the church's life and have little influence upon the respectable middle class—sometimes described as the silent majority, or the people in the pew—who silently control with their financial contributions.

The predicament for First-World churches is that the members are neither oppressed nor poor—especially when compared to the world's standards. Although not controlled by the ruling class as in Latin America, the churches in the North are dominated by the middle class and by the values that support the "middle" way of life. The churches enjoy the benefits of a democratic society and an institutional life based upon choice and voluntary participation. This has tended to foster a consensus around the broad "middle" in church values and beliefs and has given support to the broad middle way of life, free from any fundamental conflict over values. Thus the class conflict advocated by liberation education is an unlikely direction for the future of Christian educaton.

III

The liberationists also insist that the liberation model cannot be adapted to serve the current North American need for church renewal (and this can apply also to the desperate need for a *renewal* in Christian education). They believe that the question of church program must be set aside until the future of humankind and the structures of human life are resolved. The church cannot go about its usual work of nurturing a way of life that reinforces the establishment and ignores the deeper longings of those who are denied their humanity by such an establishment.

This is a strong word for a church that is faced today with institutional survival, and it is unsettling, to say the least, for the average congregation. The sense of continuity is so strong within the Western church that the issues of authority, language, governance, and even missions (priorities) are not easy to address. The reformulation of theology and the creation of fundamental new forms of faith are the burdens of liberation theology.[14]

An example of the kind of radical rethinking that is taking place is found in the writings of Penelope Washbourn. Although she writes out of feminine theology rather than the Marxist theology of the Latin Americans, she is no less confronting and demanding in her proposals for a *new* church. Her position is that the structure of governance, as well as the theology of the church, is based upon a mind-set in which some have power and authority over others and in which someone is always in a dependent relationship. Even the word *God* and the way the word is used within the life of the church serve to perpetuate this idea of dependency and allow those in authority to control the identity of individuals and the way they live in the world. The kind of radical *reform* she proposes is summarized in the following statement.

> Feminine theology for me is therefore a threat to all traditional Christian theology and church structures. It is not an attempt to "justify" the position of woman in the church and add her to the traditional Christian framework. Feminine theology is more radical than that. It calls for an end to all authoritarian models of truth, including, in my mind, the model of the ordained minister or priest, who inevitably stands in the same relationship to the laity as the divine image of God in Jesus to the followers of God.[15]

This illustrates that the issue here is the liberation of theology itself. Although we do not like to admit it, there is probably no place in the life of the church where cultural forms of faith have been as dominant as in Christian education. What Robert M. Brown has said about theology in general would be applicable to educational theology. He writes that our "perception of faith has been so strongly conditioned by our being white, middle-class Americans that in the process we have seriously distorted it."[16]

Although we can celebrate the great contributions made by the Sunday school movement, we must at the same time be aware that it has been one of the major structures for socializing the American way of life. The faith of the Sunday school was the faith of an emerging American middle class and of its longing for a better way of life. The Sunday school was a major force in the development of what has come to be known as civil religion—the equation of religious faith with the American way of life and the values of material and social success.[17]

A new *Christian consciousness* for our time is required—a consciousness that will perceive how deeply our faith is culturally bound and that will be aware of the new global dimensions of human life. Christian education must help persons learn how to form faith-statements relevant to the realities of the world in which they live. All theology is cultural, and to liberate theology is to liberate it from the passing culture, setting it free to find the new cultural context in which God is at work.

Liberation theology calls into question the very understanding of theology and of its function in Christian education. The traditional Western approach to theology has been with the *Word* rather and with the *deed*. It is a theology of books, in which the Bible is approached as a book to be read and known. Learning first about the book, theology then moves to application, or to the deed. Within Christian education, the discussion usually centers around the role of the Bible—especially how much of the Bible is to be known in order to insure that persons qualify to be Christian.

Liberation theology begins in deed. It thus provides a new understanding of the relationship between faith and action, and the content of belief and commitment. The key phrase is *theological praxis*, or the actual participation in the ongoing struggle for faith. The Bible is not a book to know in abstraction, but is the call of oppressed people to participate in the liberating acts of God the Liberator. Commitment is not to words, but to deeds that are specific and concrete.

Western theology has been generally preoccupied with

the correct propositions of faith, or with what one must believe to be truly Christian. This can be readily illustrated by the continued struggle between theological positions within Christian education, especially the ongoing debate between evangelical and liberal theologies. This is a central issue in most mainline churches, when it comes to the selection and utilization of church curriculum. For the liberation theologian, such intellectual debates are obsolete and distract from the major concern. We must engage persons in doing theology out of real social experience, rather than expending energy in abstract discussions. The issue is not the defense of the Christian faith but participation in the actions of faith that serve to clarify both the meaning and content of faith itself. As Segundo reminds us, a theology formulated within the new context of the emerging people of liberation will lead to a fresh vision and understanding of faith and to a deep and profound new experience of the Bible as Deed.[18]

Theology in all its expressions is concerned with the meanings of faith in the present social and human situation, and the way those meanings will inform the liberating experience.

Liberationists propose a mode of Christian education centering in theological practice rather than in theological words. It is an educational process which involves living from and reflecting on the deeds of faith. The implication here is that one thinks and talks about faith, not for the sake of knowing about faith, but for the sake of living for faith itself.[19]

IV

It is evident that Christian education requires a new criticalness. It has been well documented that as Christian educators, we have neglected our foundational assumptions and have adopted—at times uncritically—the assumptions and methods of general education. The early dialogue of religious education with general education led to a vitality that has long been exhausted. The crisis in the educational ministry of the church may not involve just loss of members and decline in attendance. It also involves our sense of identity and our motivation for what we do. We are not only confused as to the meaning of *Christian* when placed before *education,* but we are also at a loss as to what *education* means. Many liberationists have been critical of the hope North Americans place in education and have suggested that education really does not have the power to accomplish what is expected.

The loss of the educational mystique is best exemplified by a look at what passes for Christian education today: sensitivity training, experiential education, behavioral objectives, simulation games, self-directed learning, multimedia kits, sharing groups, and so on. This is another way of saying that education has become largely a system of techniques and methods, rather than substance (deeds of commitment are rich in knowledge). As with much of modern industrial life, education has become another element in the technocratic environment, controlling life rather than liberating it. Christian education must become liberated from education itself.

Unless we become aware of the hidden values and assumptions behind Christian education, any attempt at liberation education will be self-defeating. Both public and church education are dominated by materialistic and technological values. Look at those things we feel are essential for *good* Christian education: *paid* professional staff; buildings, with proper space allotments for each age group; equipment, including tables and chairs and technological hardware for teaching; printed resources—books, story papers, posters; an organizational structure, with teachers, superintendents, and committees. Someone has said that the crisis of the Sunday school teacher today is that there is too much material from which to choose, rather than not enough. Bureaucratic leaders inundate us with resources and guidelines, all for the cause of Christian education.

William Pinar, Herbert M. Kliebard, and others have

written about the materialistic base of current educational theory.[20] The "schooling" model of education that has been generally adopted by the church is formulated largely around managerial and industrial concepts. Not only does such an educational model assume significant financial investment but it also requires heavy use of material resources, technological tools, and electronic aids. Education is another form of "production" in which the end product is determined by behavioral objectives, and control is central to the learning process.

Schooling is therefore designed to serve the socialization needs of an industrial society and to insure that learners conform to social expectations. In order to assure conformity, the church has chosen a grading or tracking system to organize learners, has emphasized approved resources and curriculum materials, has sought to certify educational specialists, and has adopted a merchandising approach to educational programs.

Illich is right when he suggests that our very language betrays the values inherent in church education. We talk about learning systems, resource banks, superintendents and directors, learning objectives, and educational standards. Education is designed to serve the dominant minority, and through a process of certification, those who are dominated are not only eliminated but are deemed unworthy because of the lack of a certificate. Illich goes on to say that the educational system is organized to insure the role of the "technocrat" in human affairs, and it is those in charge who really benefit, not those who are supposed to be the beneficiaries.

The materialistic base for education is not only in its cost but in the way education serves to separate the haves and the have-nots. Illich writes:

> Imperceptibly all countries, East and West, have adopted a system of knowledge-capitalism. Wealth is redefined in terms of hours of instruction purchased with public funds, and poverty is explained and measured by the individual's failure to consume. In such a society the poor are those who

lag behind others in education. The rich man, the knowledge capitalist, cannot bridge the gap which separates him
from Lazarus.[21]

The quality of education has come to be based upon the
amount of money allotted to it. We have believed, even as
Christians, that salvation is determined by programs of
Christian education and that it is almost heresy to question
the allocation or to call for a more simplified and flexible
approach to the teaching of the faith and of the life to which
God calls us all. Can we, in an age of scarcity and social
injustice, continue to defend in the name of the gospel the
investment we make in educational materials and resources, and at the same time be sensitive to the plight of the
oppressed? Any new direction in church education will call
for a recovery of the central meaning of transcendence—its
meaning for the life of the whole human community.[22]

V

A new criticalness in Christian education must lead to a
reformulation of the way it functions. It will need to become
"dysfunctional" as to the way persons ordinarily live,
challenging them to become more than conscious of their
value-systems. It will be necessary for people to change
drastically the fundamental values that support the role of
the oppressor in the global society.

A style of education that is concerned with changing the
comforts of the status quo will be needed. This means
creating uncertainty in those values that are taken for
granted. Only then will persons be ready to reconstruct a
new vision for their lives.

Historically, religious education has played a significant
role in social change. There are some who would argue that
when education has become prophetic, it has successfully
challenged the popular values implicit in the life of the
church and society and has led in bringing about a new
social order. This was certainly true in the 1920s and 1930s

when religious education was instrumental in placing on the church's agenda both the rights of the laboring class and the awareness of world order. Again in the 1940s and 1950s, religious education led in breaking up the old patterns of racial isolation and establishing patterns of integration.

Prophetic education confronts the resistance to change. This requires judgment on the human condition and personal awareness of the way that judgment relates to "who I am" and "what I do." Grace, or envisioning, is also required, in the form of alternative futures that will lure persons to new choices about their lives. True prophetic education requires both judgment and grace and is incomplete when one or the other is either avoided or left out.

Persons are also motivated by visions and by a consciousness that they have a role in the future of humankind. This is the essence of the apocalyptic literature of the Bible. In the face of impending disaster, what is our hope and what is *my* role in that hope? There is no neutrality when one becomes aware of the changes the future will require and responds to the call to participate in the coming new order.

Educationally, this requires a commitment to become active in the transformation of the old order. Such transformation begins with oneself, by participation in the changes required by new order. Persons learn by acting critically toward the old order and by envisioning the new order toward which they move.

Finally, we must remember that we are Christians, who are called to serve in the coming Kingdom.[23] As Christians, we must learn to see the world through the eyes of faith. For many of us, if not for most, "faith sight" is blinded and needs to be reopened in fresh and vivid ways. We need to see the world again as Jesus would see it. This means learning to think and act as New Testament disciples.

Liberation may serve to help us learn again the story of faith and to recover the heritage of Christians who gave all they had to go into the world to serve the oppressed. The recovery of the faith-story provides the possibility for a passionate engagement with the present realities of the world and its needs. Central to church education is teaching the gospel of good news. It is here we will discover that we are delivered from dependency on the old ways and that we are free to move into a new way of life.

6

Faith Seeking Understanding: Interpretation As a Task of Christian Education

Jack L. Seymour
Carol A. Wehrheim

The thesis of this chapter is that the understanding of Christian education as an interpretation, or hermeneutical process, will provide a way to begin to resolve many of the tensions in Christian education—for example, the tension between Bible-oriented and life-oriented curricula. Jack Seymour and Carol Wehrheim also argue that Christian education can draw fearlessly on the resources of education and schooling, human-development research, or theology, as long as it addresses the more basic question of the way connections are made between life experience and faith experience. This chapter illustrates the way an interpretation approach draws on philosophical hermeneutics and biblical exegesis in defining Christian education theory and practice. It is clearly in the same tradition as the work of Groome and Wingeier.

Since Christian education has emerged as an academic field of study, a controversy has existed: Does Christian education begin with biblical understandings, or with life experience? Some have argued that knowledge of the Bible is the only proper starting point and that Christian education becomes an exploration of the content of the biblical faith. Others have argued that life experience is the proper starting point and have concluded that Christian faith must grow out of life and be meaningful to life.

This Bible-or-experience controversy has been particularly apparent in curriculum design. Many lessons advertised as biblically based begin with the Scripture narrative. Only after it has been studied and understood is application made to life. Others, advertised as Christian-life curriculum, begin with the student's emerging religious experience and seek to demonstrate how faith speaks to life issues. While biblical-curriculum designers argue that experience-based curriculum does not adequately explicate the whole of the Christian story, the experience-based writers respond that the other approach is too content-centered.

Much energy has been expended to resolve this issue, although neither position would deny that Christian faith and life need to be connected. It is the thesis of this article that the connecting of life and faith is the primary task of Christian education. Its agenda is not Bible only, or life only, but both. The task of Christian education is to engage the faith-story and the experience of living into a dialogical relationship from which meaning for living emerges.

To accomplish this task, Christian educators must seek to understand the process by which persons construct meaning in their lives. The natural process of interpreting experience and understanding its meaning provides important clues for the process of Christian education. As all education seeks to help persons make meaning, Christian education seeks to help persons make meaning in light of the revelation of the Christ of God and live faithfully in terms of that meaning. The faith-story and experience must necessarily be related. The faith-story is a tool to interpret and test one's existence, in the same way that experience helps one to understand the faith anew in different cultural epochs with different cultural needs. This chapter seeks to clarify the process of interpretation by which persons come to meaning and to describe how connections can be made between Christian faith and human experience.

Interpretation as a Task of Living

Interpretation may be the most basic of human activities. From the day one is born through each day of living, one must interpret and make sense of the cues received from the world, from other persons, from the culture, and from the transcendent.[1] These very acts of understanding the way the world, history, and others present themselves, of deciding on a response, and of acting responsibly toward another and oneself constitutes human living.

To clarify this notion, consider two persons in a conversation. Each must understand the words of the other; but merely understanding the words is not enough. Each must also seek to understand the meaning the other is attempting to communicate by the use of those words. To do so, each must listen for the emotion that carries the words, the inflection and syntax that structure the words, and the manner and body language that surround the words. Communication is a very complex operation of understanding the linguistic symbols used, the context within which they are used, and the way they are shaped by the other person's actions.

Consider also the task of infants as they are thrust into the world. The infant comes to meaning by interpreting the cues given by a caring parent, by reaching for objects about which he or she is curious, and by being brought up in the beliefs and expectations of appropriate behavior laid down by the culture.

The infant's experience of growing in meaning is an important metaphor for the process of meaning-making itself. Contemporary research, for example, suggests that as the infant acquires the ability to focus, the first object of recognition is a face, usually that of the mother. For a time, despite many other stimuli, that face seems to be all that exists in the infant's world. As focusing matures and the desire to reach out into the world expands, other stimuli are recognized as objects and called into existence. Prior to the act of recognition, the objects do not exist, or have meaning, for the child.

The process of calling into existence continues throughout life. The adolescent, for example, experiences for the first time another watching his or her actions and asks, often in panic, What does the other see? and, How do I respond?

The desire to be seen as adequate in the eyes of another carries meanings about fitting behavior. Or at the other end of life, the aging adult recalls the events of his or her life and weaves them into a story (pattern of meaning), naming the meaning for which that life has stood. In these cases, meaning comes into existence upon recognition and response—that is, by interpretation.

Throughout life, as each person is called to interpret, that person either ignores or attends to particular cues of living. The person may in fact choose to see or to ignore that which might shape his or her life. For example, during the Vietnam war many persons became so accustomed to the "body counts" announced on TV news programs that the horror and violence exhibited on the screen was ignored. It is this basic human process of interpretation that is crucial for any kind of education. Without some awareness of the reason a person responds to or ignores cues, it is impossible to discuss learning at all. When we understand how a person comes to meaning and how he or she shapes meaning, the very process of learning is uncovered.

Interpretation Theory

Philosophical hermeneutics and biblical-interpretation theory are two sources to assist the teacher in understanding this process of making meaning.[2] They address the way words, texts, and experiences carry meaning from one time to another and from one person to another. One definition of hermeneutics, that of the historian of religion Raimundo Panikkar, illustrates the complex character of the endeavor. He says that hermeneutics is "the art and science of interpretaion, of bringing forth significance, of conveying meaning, of restoring symbols to life and eventually of letting new symbols emerge. Hermeneutics is the method of overcoming the distance between a knowing subject and an object to be known."[3]

In Panikkar's definition, hermeneutics, or interpretation, is described as a process of understanding. While one task of interpretaion is to seek to understand the meaning of the texts and literary works of one's culture, another is to seek to understand the meaning present in everyday action. Both texts and experience present themselves to a person with such power that a response is called for. While it is true that interpretation theory has attended more directly to the meaning present in literary texts, this process is applicable also to contemporary experience.[4] In seeking to understand the shaping and transmission of meaning, interpretation theory leads one to consider the interpreter, the object to be interpreted, and the process of interpretation itself.

The interpreter brings his or her own frame of reference to a text or an experience. It is impossible for one to look value-free at an experience. The lens one uses is focused by one's physical and logical possibilities, by one's personal history, by one's language, and by one's motivation or need to seek to understand. For example, the preschooler at the point of individuation, who has no language to speak of separation and no way to reflect on it abstractly, is nevertheless confronted with making sense and responding to feelings. The response probably will be very concrete, perhaps narrative, in terms of experiences with parents and other loving persons. Past experiences and resources become sources for the interpretation. Therefore since the interpreter comes to an experience or text with a frame of reference, the task is to seek to understand how that frame of reference may illumine or may block the meaning that is created.

This process of coming to meaning is not as subjective as it sounds. The individual never shapes meaning in a vacuum. The interpreter is in a dynamic interaction with the world. The personal pair of glasses through which experiences are refracted into meaning is constructed by the meaning which exists externally in the world and presents itself to the person, and also by the meaning given to the individual by the stories, myths, and rituals transmitted by the culture.[5] Interpretation theory requires critical reading of the interpreter as well as of the object to be interpreted.

On the other hand, the interpretation of meaning in the

object is a complex task. Literary, or textual interpretation theory has argued that the interpreter must deal with problems of language and translation—Are the words of the text intelligible in the contemporary language of the interpreter?; with problems of context—What did these words or these stories mean in their historical frame of reference?; and with questions about the intentions of the author of the text—What did the author mean to communicate? In addition, the interpreter must deal with general questions of aesthetics, or the way a literary or artistic form might carry meaning across time. In particular, such analysis reveals that stories and symbols are able to convey different meanings to different persons in different times.

Therefore the individual brings a personal frame of reference to the discovery of meaning in a story, a work of art, or an experience, and out of this interaction new meanings emerge. It is this interaction that is the very process of interpretation. Panikkar has offered three ways to talk about this process.[6] The first he calls morphological hermeneutics, which is the explanation of life given by the elders to the young. In other words, those who have experienced the richness of a culture help the young to understand in terms of cultural meanings. It is an understanding of the present in terms of a past cultural witness to truth.

The second is diachronical hermeneutics: the attempt of one in the present to understand a text written in the past. It requires an understanding of the historical context of the text, as well as an attempt to translate its meaning to the contemporary world. The attempt to discern the meaning for the present of Paul's letters or of Augustine's *Confession* is an example. As Panikkar states, it "implies going out from my own 'stand' in order to understand another world view. . . . The movement here is from present to past in order to incorporate, subsume or delete it."[7]

The third type is diatropical hermeneutics, or the attempt to understand another culture from its own perspective. It is moving from one's own place, seeking to understand another in terms of his or her own self-understanding. This is the process of all cross-cultural communication. While it is difficult for one to step outside a personal perspective, it is possible, with patient listening and dialogue, to understand how another "sees" the world and makes sense of experience. It is a task of interpretation to attempt to see from another cultural perspective. Panikkar speaks of this attempt as coming to "stand under" the same horizon of meaning as another.

For the educator, then, the process of education is one of interpretation. It is seeking to clarify the frame of reference brought by the learner and to put it in dynamic interaction with the meanings brought by culture, by texts, and by the world itself. It is the process of bringing new meaning to birth in the interaction of learner, teacher, and wider environment. The educator also struggles with the method of education/interpretation. In some situations the educator will lead the young to experience the world in the ways the culture prescribes; in others, the educator will seek to traverse history and let the wisdom of the past speak to the present; and in still others, the educator will seek to help the learners stand in another's shoes, thereby bridging human isolation and risking communication.

Faith Seeking Understanding

When these insights are transferred to Christian education, the primary questions become the crucial ones of truthfulness: To what degree does the Christian story help us understand our experience? How does being Christian uniquely shape our way of seeing and understanding? How, in the midst of a culture, can the Christian story be told to help others understand God, world, and vocation in ways different from those the culture teaches? How do the Christian story and the cultural story shape each other? and, To what truth does the proclamation "Christ is Lord" point? The Christian educator, to use Panikkar's definition of interpretation, is called to translate the meaning of the

Christian culture to the uninitiated, to seek to understand the meanings of the Christian texts for today, and to communicate the meanings of the Christian culture so that other cultures may see the life-transforming power that is present in the Christ of God and in God's call to faithfulness in the world, in all its particularity today.[8]

The conviction upon which Christian faith stands is that life has been infused with new meaning and power because of the unique historical experience of the Christ of God. The interpretation approach recognizes that a multitude of theological traditions exists to put this experience of transcendence and transformation into understanding. It also recognizes that whenever that "event" is experienced, it must be spoken in the language and symbols of the culture. Nevertheless, the conviction remains that this event is true beyond history, language, and interpretation. A variety of theological traditions may in fact use interpretation as an approach to Christian education—to communicate how a particular history was infused with the transcendent and imminent transformation of all histories—that is, the Christ of God.[9]

For the Christian educator, the old phrase *credo ut intelligam* illustrates the crucial dynamics of the interpretation task. This phrase has been translated "faith seeking understanding." Often it has been understood as, "I believe in order that I might understand," and thus it has meant, "If I believe in the faith, I may come to understand my belief." Yet it should be translated in a much more significant manner—"I belove, or I participate fully in, in order that I might understand."[10] This reading communicates that understanding (or belief, or theology) is preceded by the experience of being made new, of being "born again." It is in the action of bringing this experience of great depth and feeling into meaning that the process of interpretation as education takes place. It is this experience of Christ that orders all other experiences. To be beloved by, and to belove the Christian experience embodied in the redemptive community, is the beginning of Christian education. This view however does not ignore the fact that one's everyday experiences and the cultures within which one lives also carry meanings that need to be integrated into one's person. The telling of the Story can provide the person with new tools to make meaning, and new cultural experiences provide occasions to understand and enrich the Story. Interpretation is an ongoing and mutual process.

Charles Winquist illustrates the process when he defines the church as a pilgrim people seeking meaning.[11] The minister (or teacher) stands as a guide within the church, attending to the Spirit which infuses it with meaning. For Winquist, the task of the ministry of interpretation is fourfold: (1) to accept the experience of another; (2) to invite that experience into dialogue with the story of the faith; (3) to mediate the meaning present in Christian stories, symbols, and rituals; and (4) to imagine with another the action demanded as that experience is now "re-meaned," re-symbolized and re-told through the power of the Christian faith.

Christian education, therefore, is attending to the power of transformation presented in an experience through the gift of the Spirit of God, mediated by Christian story and symbol and embodied in a redefined vocation for living in the world in a particular historical epoch. After such an act of interpretation, a person's life is transformed. New images, new connections, and new decisions are made.[12] The experiences of life are seen as potentially revelatory of the greater meaning in life itself.

Teacher: Guide for the Journey

The teacher has a crucial role to play in this understanding of Christian education. The teacher functions as a guide for the learner who is on a pilgrimage toward meaning. While the teacher is clearly someone who knows something of the way, he or she travels with the learner, rather than standing ahead, beckoning, as someone who has already completed the journey; or behind, pushing the learner on, as someone who does not need to go on this journey. The teacher risks participation in a mutual journey with the learner and by so doing, acts as model. Thomas Groome suggests that the teacher be named "leading learner."[13]

The primary function of the guide who is involved in a journey of meaning is to make decisions and recommendations about what is needed for the journey. Just as fur-lined parkas would not be important to a group of hikers on the Appalachian Trail in August, neither would a section on the sacraments from Calvin's *Institutes* be particularly helpful to a group of kindergarteners learning about baptism. The process of guidance, using the faith-story as a lens, can be accomplished in a myriad of ways. Decisions about the process might be likened, holding to the analogy of the travel guide, to the selection of the best route for the travelers. However, it is the travelers themselves who have chosen to make the journey. The guidance process is a mutual one.

The teacher uses the power of creative imagination to guide.[14] The task is to recall the story of the faith and to help the student make the connections. Here interpretation interacts with the other approaches described in this volume. A teacher could hardly make decisions about needed resources without an understanding of the developmental stages, the theology and practice of the Christian religion, or perhaps the particular nature of that community of faith. However, the primary methodological question is this: What resources are needed to help this student along this path?

To use the words of the tradition, the teacher has the duties of sage, prophet, and priest.[15] As sage, the teacher seeks with the learner to delve the depths of the personal meanings which are brought to bear on experience. A very painful and critical analytic process can result from the discovery of hidden psychological blocks to understanding and personal inadequacies. As prophet, the teacher proclaims the faith tradition, asking whether the meanings one makes of an experience are faithful to or revelatory of the ultimate Meaning in the universe. Finally, the teacher is priest, bringing healing to those wounds, opening up the student to the world of Spirit and symbol, and sanctifying the experience by helping to connect it to the power in the Christian story and symbol. The process moves from recalling the surface understandings made of experience, critically understanding personal limitations, and reconnecting the experience to a deeper level of meaning, in contact with the power of transcendence.

To be involved in such a process of criticism and renewal takes some particular characteristics on the part of the teacher. These characteristics, or gifts of the Spirit, seem central. First, teachers would be willing to hazard their own reflections and interpretations. But they would continually acknowledge them as their own. Thus they would not only model a way to reflect and to interpret, but they would exhibit a willingness to risk and to change, which marks the journey of faith.

A second characteristic is the teacher's critical awareness of his or her own assumptions and presuppositions. Unless this characteristic is present and the teacher's own assumptions are frequently examined, it is easy for interpretation to disintegrate into a personal formula for viewing the world which is not open to the new that emerges from each encounter of experience and traditions.

Third, the teacher allows and, indeed, encourages students to do their own reflection and interpretation. Questions are asked to promote searching and discussion rather than to provide a format for giving correct answers. That the students have choices, and thereby decisions to make, is honored. While their choices may not be the teacher's choice, the teacher recognizes that the choices may be their way of infusing life with new meaning.

Fourth, it is important that the teacher accept the lives and experiences of the students as valid. Frequently it is necessary for a group of learners to participate in a common experience, reflecting and interpreting together, and thereby enriching for all the quality of both the interpretation and the experience. If, however, the reflection and interpretation does not at some point touch the everyday lives of the learners, both the experience and the faith-story will remain in once-a-week or done-at-church memories. So the teacher must be someone who values the lives and experiences of the students in a way that includes those lives and experiences in the learning and gives value to them.

The Learner: Pilgrim in Search of Meaning

The learner can be best understood as a pilgrim in search of meaning and vocation. Building on past experiences and utilizing personal interpretative skills, the learner seeks to make connections that will provide clues for meaningful living.

An examination of the actual practice of Christian pilgrimage will clarify the role of the learner in Christian education. Victor Turner, the noted anthropologist, has carefully described Christian pilgrimage practices.[16] It is his argument the Christian pilgrimage is a ritual process by which the pilgrim separates himself or herself from everyday understandings and enters a new stage of living, open to an in-depth experiencing of the faith.

In Christian pilgrimage, the pilgrim imitates Jesus' free submission of his will to the direction of God. It begins with the conscious decision of the pilgrim to give up for a time "not only the cares but also the rewards of ordinary life" and to undertake an often perilous journey, one filled with thieves, natural dangers, and epidemics.[17]

On the pilgrimage, one meets fellow pilgrims who also are engaging in a search for meaning. Together these pilgrims encounter Christian symbols, immerse themselves in the tradition, and open themselves to the presence of God. Through the experience, they are transformed. "The doors of perception" are revised and vision is redirected. Some previously important assumptions are relativized, and with new eyes, experience is opened to the presence of

God.[18] Not only are the pilgrims better able to state the meaning of the experience of the God of Jesus—that is, to do theology—but each is redirected. Experiences are encountered in a new way, in light of "re-newed" perspectives. A Christian pilgrim returns to ordinary life filled with a new vision, a new perception, and a new call to vocation.

To translate this experience into Christian education, the learner willingly risks the normal perspective of everyday life and seeks to understand from the perspective of Christian tradition. Many of the usual ways of understanding experience are shattered by the view of the tradition. New symbols are allowed to operate, explaining and structuring experience. In fact, one comes to view experiences *sub species aeternitatis* ("in light of eternity"). In this manner, experience is brought beyond the mundane and given new meaning. The learner struggles with what the Christian tradition and the experience of Christ have to say to the experience of the learner.

As in pilgrimage, this process is very dangerous. The individual encounters the psychological equivalent of thieves and famine on the journey toward meaning. By suspending the ordinary frame of reference, or ordinary tasks, one not only opens oneself up to the possibility of revelation, but also to the shattering of the very foundation upon which one stands. One also must be careful that the connections or new meanings made are in fact warranted and true to both experience and tradition. Without care, it is possible to be misled and follow a direction that might not be productive for faithful vocation.

However, as in pilgrimage, the learner encounters others who also are seeking to make the connections between faith and life. The search for meaning in light of the experience of Christ thus becomes a mutual exploration. The community of faith can become a setting where persons share their own experiences, their insights, their concern for one another, and their attempts to respond faithfully to God's ongoing revelation within life. The church itself is a company of pilgrims in search of meaning and vocation.

Process and Content

It is impossible to describe only one process of interpretation. Different skills are needed for each of the interpretation agendas. However, unifying factors may be discussed in any interpretation process.

Morphological hermeneutics, for example, requires skills to help the uninitiated see their experiences in light of the Christian world-view for the first time. The skills most needed here are those of listening and proclamation. The teacher needs to listen to the story of the experience of the learner and to proclaim the Christian story as an alternative way of understanding.

Skills required for diachronical hermeneutics are primarily those of textual criticism and exegesis. Certainly the first task is to uncover the context of the original text and to attempt to discuss the meaning it had in its time. Historical critical tools are extremely useful. Yet the subsequent connection of the meaning of a past text to the present is not easily done, and here is where historical analysis has been found to be limited. Merely to know what an object meant in its own time does not insure that it can be connected to the present. Creative play of the imagination is necessary for such connections.[19]

Diatropical hermeneutics is the most difficult. It requires skills of cross-cultural communication. Both teacher and learner are challenged to give up their "superior" feeling in order to participate in the self-understanding of the other. Listening is of crucial significance. One must listen to an experience in the life of the other, mutually engage in dialogue about the self-understandings, and seek to understand the new truth that emerges from this encounter. Both trust and a willingness to risk are essential for this process; it requires ultimate faith in one's own perspective as well as a tentative hold on that perspective. One must trust that the truth to which his or her faith points will in fact be illumined more carefully by the mutual dialogue, even though some of the words and symbols used to express that truth will be challenged and found wanting. To refer again to developmental theory, a particular stage of adult maturity is required for this hermeneutic to be possible.

Some of the overlapping factors in any process of interpretation are the following: (1) honoring the experience of the other; (2) listening for multiple levels of meaning; (3) mediation of Christian symbol and story; and (4) dialogue and decision.[20] Any interpretation process begins with honoring the experience of the other, whether the experience be told orally or recorded in written or visual form. Experience itself is the birth of meaning. An experience may be an encounter, a dream, a fantasy, or the hearing of a story. It is that which presents the depth and variety to be found in human life, as the phrase "faith seeking understanding" communicates the act of beloving, or "participation" precedes that of analysis or meaning-making. One recognizes the importance of an experience, but only by understanding it in terms of story (whether Christian or cultural) and symbol does it gain meaning and real significance. Panikkar has also expressed this insight: "Without hermeneutics myth and faith would perish the moment that the innocence of the ecstatic attitude passes away."[21] Experience is the context within which God continues to act, and the message of God must be understandably spoken. Within experience, justice is enacted, theophanies occur, and resurrection brings new life.

Second, listening to the presentation of experience is important. Persons need to be helped to see the meaning they automatically project onto experience. By this act, personal foundational convictions are revealed. A teacher must understand that these convictions may be potentially either insightful or concealing. The attitudes taken toward these meanings must then be both respect and suspicion. Questions must be asked about what these meanings reveal and whether they are adequate. For example, the simple word spoken by a child during a parents' argument may reveal for both parents the context of love that unites them. On the other hand, sexist language used in a worship service may conceal the feminine side of God and the unity of all humans. The action of careful respect and suspicion may celebrate the truth one has learned, or it may prophetically point one to a truth to which one has been blind. Listening to the multiple levels of meaning reveals insight as well as issues for spiritual reflection.

Third, the story and symbol of Christian faith are to be mediated into the learner's perspective by the guidance of the teacher. Although each individual must make sense of his or her experiences and test the veracity of the interpretation in the midst of life's actions, the individual is limited to the stories and symbols to which he or she has access. The Christian educator believes that the Christian experience of redemption in Christ, symbolized in ritual actions and icons, stated in narratives, and clarified in theology offers a unique and meaningful way to understand everyday life and to raise it to ultimate significance. Without contact with Christian stories and symbols, the learner is limited in understanding the experience. An example of this truth is seen in the Gospel stories which tell of the miraculous actions Jesus performed, such as casting out demons. Only those who had the eyes to see (those who had the story and symbols to interpret the experience as a miracle of God) could observe it. Others thought Jesus was a magician or of the devil, and only those who believed (who had received the story of God's new act in Christ) saw Jesus as the Christ. The mediation and clarification of the Christian faith offers new light on experience. Yet this action is always accomplished in dynamic interaction with the story and symbol of the culture providing the context in which the transcendent is particularly embodied.

Sharing in story and symbol is much more than an academic and cognitive activity. Interpretation is not merely an explanation of an experience or of a text. The parables, in fact, were interpretations of everyday life which, through their narrative quality, brought new meanings into view. They were simultaneously event and interpretation. A teacher needs to be continually aware of the power of parable, narrative, art, symbol, or myth to reveal a depth dimension in an experience. Therefore, while much attention is given to doing theology on experience, just as much needs to be given to imagination, fantasy, ritual, story, and symbol as ways to clarify and mediate the originating Christian experience.

Dialogue and decision are the last stages in the process. Within a setting of trust, the learner has revealed experience to self and to others—a guide or a learning group. The others in turn have risked their own meaning in encounter. In dialogue, alternative symbols and stories, tacit agreements, and personal histories are brought to bear on the experience to discover the meaning it might have. Some understandings have been found lacking and others have seemed to offer insight. In the last analysis, it is the learner who must choose how he or she will make meaning of an experience. Yet the others can be of great assistance in the dialogue of meanings and in the decision of meaning. It is the act of deciding that is the culmination of the process. To interpret an experience in a particular way is to respond to it in a particular action. It is impossible to think of the search for meaning as being separated from action; one leads into and demands the other. The action one takes is dependent upon one's interpretation.

Of course, while interpretation is demanded of all people in relation to all experiences, it is impossible and would be inadvisable to reflect on all experiences. For some experiences, the interpretation is clear: It is reflex, such as steering the wheels of a car to avoid a collision or pushing a child out of the way of a falling object. But to reflect on the meaning of those experiences that significantly affect identity and community is to offer new possibilities for both. The Christian educator knows that each experience ultimately can point to the event of Christ and hopes that persons can come to see their lives in light of the faith. Yet the educator also knows that the event of Christ must be "re-meaned" in stories and symbols appropriate to a particular context.

The process and content of Christian education therefore suggest that we at least honor experience, reflect critically upon it, link it to the story and symbol of the faith, and from it, choose mission and vocation.

Conclusion: On Shaping an Interpretive Community

The implications of this understanding of Christian education for individual and small-group settings in education and ministry are relatively clear. It provides the "leading learner" not only with a process of teaching, but with a self-understanding. It also has profound implications for the church's total educative ministry. This approach provides a self-understanding and direction for church efforts at education.

Seen as a community endeavor, the task of education is not so much that of adjusting educational programs, as attending to the educative dimensions throughout the church's ministry. The educator must begin by interpreting the experiences of the life of church—both educational programs and total ministry—in relation to Christian experience. Primary questions will concern the faithfulness of the church, the way persons are helped on their journeys toward meaning and vocation, and how this community makes the connection between life and faith, which renews both. The church as the company of pilgrims in search of meaning and vocation becomes the context for educational ministry. Christian education cannot be relegated to particular segments of ministry or confined to discrete groupings of church people, although it can use a variety of these segments and groups in designing an educational program.

While there is no one way to describe an interpretive community, we may obtain hints by looking at some of the items on the weekly calendar of a church that attempts to be an interpretive community. That calendar lists the following events:

  —church school classes on Sunday morning. Some of these are organized not only by age group but by life experiences. One such group is for persons (of all ages) who recently have moved or who soon will move. They will consider that experience in light of both the Exodus and the command of Jesus to go into the world.

—Outreach Committee meeting. Members are to share their personal reasons for being involved in this ministry of the church.

—Education Committee meeting. Members are to bring the reports of interviews with children in the junior class of the church school.

—worship on Sunday morning. The text for the sermon was given the previous week, with questions to ponder. (This information was also in the church newsletter and in an ad in the local newspaper.)

—Senior High Group. Discussion with officials of the county government about clean-air standards, as a result of a study unit on ecology and stewardship.

—pastor's meeting with a student in the congregation to discuss vocation. The student has been denied admission to a desired academic program.

—special celebration of the twenty-fifth anniversary of the church to examine the purposes that have guided the church. In planning for this evening, the committee sought to answer how God has been present in the church's life and where God is leading the church.

—meeting with public school teachers in the congregation to discuss problems they are having in the schools and assist the church in a decision about a response to the problems.

Such a listing builds on the strengths that are already present in the church program and focuses more sharply some of the activities that maintain the life of the church and that also lead it into mission. Attention is given to making connections between faith and life.

As educational decisions are made, it is recognized that church members bring with them a variety of experiences, as well as ideas, impressions, and knowledge of the

Christian faith. In particular, their knowledge of the faith-story may come from a childhood Sunday school class, television religion, or a parent's faith. Their central values and convictions may be drawn from their place of work, school, or ethnic heritage, more than from the Christian heritage. This experience and knowledge is seriously considered, for it is out of this that persons make sense of their lives and decide on appropriate action. Attention is given to making intersections with these personal contexts for learning, so that their power can be acknowledged, judged, expanded, or honored. The degree to which church life is purposive and the agendas of church members are heard and confronted is crucial.

In an interpretive community, the educational ministry is built around arenas of life and meaning. Four are particularly important: (1) the faith-story; (2) personal, spiritual experience; (3) cultural experience; and (4) practice of ministry. The educational ministry is structured to address each arena and provide occasions for integration.

The educator asks: Where in the church's ministry is the pilgrim acquiring an understanding of the Christian texts and faith-story? Where is the student's personal spiritual experience being addressed? Where is the cultural experience of each learner, as well as the wider cultural context, being confronted? Where is the ministry of each person being supported, encouraged, and assessed? The answers will be found in a variety of settings throughout the life and ministries of the church, but the educator needs to know how and where they are occurring in order to create a coordinated relationship. For example, the faith-story may best be learned in a church school classroom; the spiritual experience, through a spiritual direction group; the cultural context, in church committee meetings and in events that unite persons around common experiences and interests; the ministering experience, in individual and small-group spiritual direction, and even in the church council's reevaluation of the church's mission. The educator will see that each arena is addressed and that individuals are guided as they move through them.

Such an understanding of Christian education requires a significant program of leadership training. Persons who are able to plan for and shape an interpretive community and teachers who are capable of guiding the process of interpretation are essential. Our usual processes of training educational leaders and teachers do not emphasize these particular skills, but focus more on planning the church's formal educational program and on teaching skills. A different starting point for this model might involve training persons in the process of interpretation by focusing on their own experience in the church's life and program.

It will take time and effort to shape an interpretive community. It must be brought into being and nurtured by persons who struggle to make connections between the gospel and life. In this way, Christian education becomes a servant of the church, and of Christian experience, by enabling the church's mission and Christian living. The natural process of living, by which meaning is clarified and decisions about life-style and vocation are made, is infused with the power of the transformatory experience of the Christ. Shaping such a community will be difficult, but it is precisely the task needed to support Christian faith in a pluralistic environment, and its results can significantly alter the whole life of the church.

7

The Future of Christian Education
Donald E. Miller
Jack L. Seymour

Attempting to project the future is always a dangerous activity. It usually reveals more about those who shape the projection than about the future. Nevertheless, it is the process of dreaming which defines the questions that will be addressed and reveals some of the resources for encountering the future.

Consider, for example, the varying dreams which motivated Christian education at the beginning of the twentieth century. While some educators triumphally claimed that the Sunday school had reached the pinnacle of success, encircling the world with the Christian message, others dreamed that the Sunday school would be replaced by a real school, which would stand as the equal of the public school in conception, method, and effect. Still others hoped that more attention would be given to enriching the natural occasions when persons shared the faith with one another and grew in understanding and faithfulness. Christian education was variously seen as a school, a home, an educational system, a mission agency, and as a school for Christian living. These dreams revealed the conflicts Christian education was to face throughout much of the twentieth century; yet they also clarified its resources and motivated efforts on its behalf.

It is our attempt in this chapter to examine the agenda, resources, and hopes for Christian education. We will not produce a description of the future, as much as we will clarify a pathway into that future. After analyzing the contributions of each of the approaches explored in this volume and the concerns raised, issues for the future of

Christian education will be defined. By attention to these issues, the search for an appropriate identity and form for Christian education will be continued.

Contemporary Approaches to Christian Education

The underlying metaphors that have guided the selection of materials for this book are being developed in various ways by different educators in our time. Each metaphor takes a particular shape according to the vision of a given interpreter. Let us review the particular interpretations given by the writers of the various chapters of this book. We will look especially at the basic elements of the guiding metaphors as they have been presented, in order to rehearse both the points of agreement and the points of tension. We believe that the future of Christian education in our generation will be shaped to a great degree by the way these guiding metaphors agree and disagree.

Sara Little believes that religious instruction deals with religious subject matter by enabling the learners to assess the truth within their own frames of reference. This view is sharply distinguished from a view of instruction in which the responses of the learners are assessed from the standpoint of the teacher. These two views are not necessarily opposed, at least as long as the vantage point of student and teacher coincide, but the second might turn into a form of coercion. Sara Little clearly separates herself from that kind of instruction, which could be called training, conditioning, or indoctrination. Such views elevate the vantage point of the teacher and depreciate respect for the student.

Instruction takes place during moments of understanding, deciding, and believing. The teacher organizes and guides learning activities, but the center of instruction is always the responsiveness of the student. In the moments of understanding, deciding, and believing, there is no final separation between teaching and learning. The "teacher" is always learning anew in the process, and the "learners" are teaching themselves and one another.

To understand is to re-present and think clearly about the meaning and the coherence of the subject matter—the religious heritage. Clear thinking is the basis for evaluation and decision. Correspondingly, deciding is always based upon underlying core beliefs (a religious community actually lives at the level of core beliefs).

Such a view of instruction is clearly complementary, at many points, to other images of education presented in this book. It presumes a religious community where core beliefs, worship, traditions, and Scripture are the subject matter for careful thinking. It allows for developmental and other individual differences among the learners. It seems to suggest that right thinking about the tradition may lead to critical evaluation of the surrounding culture, and therefore instruction may also be prophetic. The heart of such instruction is interpretation and decision.

On the other hand, certain tensions are not difficult to discover. If Charles Foster believes that certain shifting beliefs in the contemporary world are undermining the sense of community, they are equally undermining the possibility of instruction as Sara Little conceives it. The very struggle with teacher-centered instruction throughout her chapter belies the overwhelming and almost customary orientation of many Sunday schools to training and indoctrination. To state the matter in a more affirmative fashion, let us ask whether a group of largely untrained teachers, meeting with students forty minutes each week, really can stimulate clear thinking. Because the instructional model is working so poorly in so many places, commentators such as Westerhoff have turned to the noninstructional teaching functions of the congregation.

The reluctance to learn is a central theme of some developmentalists. People do not willingly seek to understand, nor do they easily allow their core beliefs to be altered. Resistance to learning and understanding is as characteristic of people as is genuine learning. Furthermore, a liberation perspective insists that we may be deceiving ourselves when we believe that we are thinking clearly. We may be simply rationalizing our privilege. Can one understand before the will has been converted?

Perhaps these tensions may serve to highlight the importance of good instruction. The respect for persons, for the renewal of community, for expression, for change, and for truth—each is a part of instruction as presented here. The search for truth is not the sole possession of the highly trained. And shifting cultural values and privileged values may be just the subject matter about which the religious community is to think more clearly. The tensions are not thereby resolved, but instruction rightly conceived can be a powerful influence in the future of Christian education.

The concept of the faith community, as Charles Foster conceives of it, involves a number of elements: (1) an originating event; (2) persons who are joined in a common spontaneous response to the event; (3) the original event relived in a variety of ways; and (4) the responses adapted to contemporary circumstances. There are a variety of ways to relive an event: storytelling, celebrating, evaluating and deciding together, engaging in activities and programs, and more.

Within this concept Christian education takes on the character of nurture. Relationships, collective experiences, and responses are essential. Instruction as conceived by Sara Little may fit nicely with this concept of the faith community, but instruction is not essential to it. Remembrance, celebration, relationship, and spontaneous response can be experienced without the effort of right thinking. In the extreme, understanding may be reduced to storytelling; valuing and deciding, to uncritical spontaneous expression. But while instruction may be included, it is also disposable.

Similarly, the concept of development can fit nicely with such a conception. The reliving and common response to a past event may be carried out within the limits of the life state of each respondent. Such interaction also may serve to stimulate the development of persons toward greater maturity. Yet there are certainly some tensions between this concept of community and the concept of development. A really common response to an originating event would be at the lowest stage level of development, since higher level responses could not be common to those of lower stages. Such a community, as is often true in congregational life, blocks maturity rather than stimulates it. The concept of development accounts for persons' possible resistance to participation, something not accounted for in Foster's view of community. So development and community may be set against each other in a particular congregation or religious group.

In a similar way, the concept of community is not intrinsically contradictory to the concept of liberation. Liberation as Freire and others practice it involves the building of "base communities" which study their common oppression and work together for their common release. This could be done within the framework of the reliving of an original liberating event. Spontaneous and evaluative responses could take into account contemporary oppression and hoped-for release. Yet again we find underlying tensions. The originating event may be interpreted as the self-justification of privilege rather than as the liberation of the oppressed. The reliving and the response may simply clothe the extension of culture religion and local custom. This view of community can contribute to the denial of liberation rather than its enhancement. The two concepts are not inherently contradictory, but the possibility for contradiction is very great. We can expect that the concept of the faith community will continue with this tension in the future.

The concept of development as formulated by Donald Miller includes these elements: (1) ground plan; (2) invariant sequence; (3) a *telos*, or goal; (4) interaction with the environment; and (5) levels of increasing complexity. While other writers have suggested that the first three elements are sufficient, Miller argues for the inclusion of the latter two. Emotional, moral, and cognitive elements are gathered together in the developmental approach.

This concept of faith development could fit nicely with

Sara Little's notion of religious instruction; understanding, deciding, and believing could be appropriated at each stage of spiritual growth. Faith development also can occur within the faith community, with all persons reliving past events and responding spontaneously according to their own life stages and circumstances. Liberation and awareness of oppression could be adapted to the faith development of persons and communities. Interpretation of life events could be adapted to persons' cognitive and moral development. The concept is not intrinsically contradictory to other points of view.

But there can be very sharp tensions within the concept and between concepts. Many educators follow a more limited view of development, highlighting the ground plan, sequence, and goal. The result can be highly individualistic and deeply inward, thus losing the interactional character of Miller's concept. Nor is the concept clear as to how far a person matures, why maturation is arrested, and whether a person can regress.

We have already alluded to the tension between development on the one hand, and instruction and faith community on the other. The contrast with liberation is sharper. Development can be a characteristic of communities as well as of individuals. The liberation concept contradicts the view that the movement toward justice is an easy and natural one. Development has been used too long as a justification for the interest of the more powerful and privileged. Liberation calls for radical transformation, rather than approximation along a sequence of stages. In that sense, the liberation of a community is like the radical conversion of an individual.

The concept of liberation as presented by Allen Moore has several essential elements: (1) awareness of systemic injustice; (2) common commitment to a life-style that liberates from systemic injustice; and (3) reformation of church structures to eliminate systemic injustice. We also could mention the reformation of church schooling to eliminate its sanction of oppression-producing values. However, this latter point is implicit in the third element.

Liberation stands in sharpest contrast to the other concepts being discussed here, but it does not always flatly contradict the others. The instructional moments of understanding, valuing, and believing can be entirely consonant with the liberation moments of awareness, life-style choice, and reforming. However, the identification and action involvement to eliminate systemic injustice is essential to liberation, and unless instruction focuses upon such awareness and such action, there will in fact be a clear contradiction.

And there is no intrinsic contradiction between liberation and the concept of community. The faith community's originating event, response, and adaptation may very well be liberation's awareness, commitment, and reformation. The faith community's originating event, however, must be understood and relived as the overcoming of systemic injustice—any other interpretation would stand in clear contradiction to liberation. Liberation educators are highly critical of concepts of the faith community that do not include the elimination of systemic injustice; they see many practices of churches as being culture-bound, self-serving, and supportive of injustice.

Similar observations can be made about the concepts of spiritual development and interpretation. Here there may be a clear contradiction. Development presumes successive movements toward growth, while liberation presumes radical transformation. Unless liberation can allow that oppression may be differently perceived and understood at different levels of maturity, or unless development can allow that any successive stage may be a total contradiction of the previous one, or unless some combination of these two possibilities is allowed, there is no way for the two concepts to be brought into logical agreement. Hence the sharp criticism of the concept of development by liberation educators.

Interpretation may well include a moment of critical awareness of systemic injustice and may therefore fit nicely with the concept of liberation. But such critical awareness is not highlighted in the description of interpretation education as presented by Jack Seymour and Carol Wehrheim, and in practice, it may not be included. Liberation educators point out that the hermeneutical approach is usually as culture-bound and oppressive as other models.

The basic elements of the presented concept of interpretation are these: (1) communicating through interaction; (2) eliciting the multiple symbols in human experience; (3) identifying and connecting the multiple symbols of the religious tradition; and (4) creating new symbols in the interaction between present experience and religious tradition.

The interpretation, or hermeneutical, approach relates easily to instruction. Understanding, valuing, and believing are all there. Jack Seymour and Carol Wehrheim's concept of interpretation does not make right thinking as central as does Sara Little's view of instruction, but right thinking could easily be included in interpretation. Interpretation could be, and probably is, frequently done without great concern about right thinking. So clearly, a tension may exist between these approaches.

The interpretation approach also interlocks nicely with the faith community. Since interpretation entails human communication, there is an implied community. Unless the original community-creating event is some kind of muted uninterpreted intuition, interpretation will always be present in community. The two concepts do fit together, although the faith community as presented puts the priority upon the spontaneity of the response, while the concept of interpretation emphasizes the resymbolization of experience. There is an obvious tension between symbolization and spontaneity which could lead to a struggle such as the one described in I Corinthians 14.

Interpretation and development need not contradict each other. Resymbolization could take place within the limits of cognitive development, and symbolization could attend to the dynamics of emotional development. Since faith development as described by Donald Miller has a definable cognitive element, the role of symbols, and therefore of interpretation, is very important. The presentation of interpretation always refers to the actual symbolic system of the learner, so that implicitly developmental problems are being addressed. Nevertheless, the interpretive approach does not imply careful attention to the sequence and goal of cognitive development. In the extreme, it may reject developmental considerations as irrelevant. On the other hand, development depends more upon peer interaction, while the resymbolization process of interpretation surely requires a teacher. We conclude that there is a subtle tension between interpretation and development.

The relationship between interpretation and liberation is more quixotic; there may be either a radical contradiction or a radical coincidence. When interpretation is imprisoned within class values and cultural privilege, liberation educators reject it; but these same educators are much concerned about symbolic interpretation and resymbolization. In other words, when interpretation focuses awareness of and response to oppression, and when it is tied to action (praxis) as well as conceptualization, then the principles of interpretation are very complementary to liberation.

These guiding metaphors relate to one another and contradict one another in important ways. Their points of agreement and tension denote crucial issues for the future of Christian education.

Agenda for the Future

The prospect for the future does not depend upon our accepting one of these contemporary approaches and remaking Christian education along its lines. Rather, it is dependent upon our remaining aware of the possibilities and problems of the various approaches as we make our formative choices. We offer five directions that may stimulate the shaping of Christian education: (1) Christian education must seek to recover its historic commitment to social transformation; (2) Christian educators must continue to define Christian education as a central yet distinct ministry of the church; (3) the relationship of developmental psychological theory to Christian education must be reconsidered; (4) Christian educators must seek to clarify the relationship of Christian education to the wider learning environment; (5) the foundational relationship of Christian education to both educational theory and theology must be explored continually.

1. *Christian education must seek to recover its historic commitment to social transformation.*

While the concern for social transformation has pervaded the movements for Christian education in America, Christian education practice has not always fulfilled this agenda. More often it has functioned purely to maintain the life of the congregation or to funnel new members into the church, thereby falling victim to the privatized and civil character of religion in American society. Today it is important to reclaim the prophetic stance of Christian education.

The early conception of the Sunday school included a moral education agenda. It was believed that by teaching children the "four Rs" of reading, writing, arithmetic, and religion, society could be transformed and some children saved from lives of poverty. Such a vision continued to inspire mission Sunday schools until late in the nineteenth century. Also, the Religious Education Association was born in 1903 with a vision of the way religion affected the shape of public life. While these visions have not always been realized and too often have deteriorated into the uncritical inculcation of middle-class values, Christian education has time and again significantly addressed the common life. It has been permeated with a conviction that the world can experience the effects of the God of history and that the faithful can cooperate with God in the humanization of life, in light of the vision of the Kingdom.

This vision is no less needed today. Christian educators find themselves faced with a pluralistic religious environment where many of the triumphal values that have motivated their work are no longer operative, and as prosperous Christians, they are faced with critical questions of faithfulness and life-style. In fact, the situation for Christianity today is much like that of the Hebrews during the period of Solomon, when there were great temptations to merge the faith with alien cultures, and corresponding attempts to criticize that merger prophetically, as well as an impending sense of the downfall of culture.

Christian education must continue to address questions about the agenda for Christian mission and vocation—questions raised by the present situation of the world, with its hunger, oppression, and gap in wealth—and about how to speak the Christian message meaningfully and powerfully in this cultural context.

This does not mean that Christian educators must forget or ignore all they have learned about personal transformation. Yet it does mean that the individual agenda must be balanced with attention to the social context for learning, as well as with the place of Christian education in the mission of the church. Attention should be given to building an approach to Christian education which understands how persons are formed in a social context and how a responsible commitment to the wider world can be built.

The vision of the Kingdom inspires hope for a world of unity, freedom, relationship, and justice. It is a dealienating vision, which motivates efforts at both personal and social transformation. The task of addressing the questions of faithfulness to the Kingdom and of development of a faithful style of living is crucial and foundational for Christian education in the present and into the future.

2. *Christian educators must continue to define Christian education as a central yet distinct ministry of the church.*

While Christian educators have continually argued that education is a ministry and must be united with a holistic understanding of the ministry of the church, the typical experience has been that education is segmented from the total life of the church into a church-school-and-fellowship program. Such a separation of education and ministry ignores crucial tasks in the life of the congregation. The contemporary expression of the faith community approach has reaffirmed this insight. Those who care about the church must ask how persons can hear the Christian message, how the faith will be transmitted to the next generation, and how believers can grow in understanding and faithfulness. Critics may claim that the typical church school programs are ineffective; nevertheless, vehicles must be found to carry the church's ministry of education if Christian persons are to be formed, grow in faithfulness, and attempt to embody the Christian faith in their lives.

The unity of ministry must be addressed. The proclamation of the Word, care for individuals, response to social conditions, growth in understanding, individual spiritual maturation, and worship of God—all these coalesce in our attempt to respond to God's presence in the world and to be agents of God's kingdom. Yet the distinctive characteristics of the task areas of ministry must also be identified, as well as the way they relate to each other. Some contemporary Christian education theorists, for example, have so blurred the lines between these task areas that the particular contribution of each is lost.

To state the two tasks of educational ministry as *apologetics* and *guidance* helps to clarify this distinctive relationship. Apologetics is crucial in any age of pluralism. Then Christianity stands alongside other interpretations of experience. If its message does not seem to interpret experience adequately, it will be dismissed as unimportant. As the Israelites sought to state their faith cogently in the Diaspora, and as early church theologians took part in dialogue with the Greco-Roman world, today's Christians must seek to clarify the meaning of the Christ-event in a world that will be increasingly bombarded with alternative religious and secular perspectives on life. That may be the primary educational task for the next generation: to clarify the message and to seek ways for the event of Christ to be experienced and understood as meaningful.

The apologetic task leads directly to that of guidance. Persons need to be helped to understand the meaning of life. Christians believe that connections must be made between everyday experience and the experience of the faith. Again, in a pluralistic era it is increasingly difficult to see these connections; there are so many ways to resolve the question of meaning. For one to be a Christian and to grow in understanding and faithfulness, one must know the ways that other Christians throughout history have attempted to understand the meaning of the revelation of God through Jesus the Christ; and to interpret life, one must acquire a set of lenses formed out of that Christian story. While some past formulations will be found lacking, and new cultural experiences will help persons understand the message in new ways, the task of interpreting life in light of Christian faith will continue as a primary educational task. The Christian teacher, in mutuality with the student, will be a guide in the search for meaning and vocation.

Such an agenda demands clarification of the educational roles of teacher and pastor. Both apology and guidance, as well as the development of a holistic praxis of ministry, require religious and ministerial leadership skills.

The teacher is more than a technician who applies certain skills to achieve certain outcomes. The teacher is one who struggles *with* the learner to discover the meaning and mission that God is attempting to reveal. Discerning the presence and meaning of God in life is an essential part of Christian education. Teaching, therefore, is professing the faith, caring for another, and guiding that other person in discernment of Christian life and vocation. While attention could well be given to the skills needed for teaching, even more attention should be directed to understanding Christian teaching as a religious and ministerial vocation.

This is also true for the pastoral role. The Reformed and Puritan understandings of the pastor were filled with the imagery of teaching. The pastor was to be a shepherd who guided the faithful and taught the faith. Today, teaching and educational leadership seem to have been omitted from the pastoral self-understanding. Frankly, the lack of attention to the religious character of teaching may have been a primary cause for this omission. Pastoral leadership is necessary for the development of a holistic ministry which incorporates understanding of the faith and decision about Christian action.

Christian education is an essential ministry, but like all other task areas, it has a distinctive agenda. Much work has yet to be done in clarifying the relationships among its distinctive and holistic tasks.

3. *The relationship of developmental psychological theory to Christian education must be reconsidered.*

In the last century, Christian education has been greatly influenced by the progress in developmental psychology. In fact, some have argued that at times Christian education theory has been little more than developmental psychology. While the relationship has been productive, helping Christian educators understand both the processes by which content can be sequenced and the developmental crises individuals must face, the relationship between growth as defined by development and growth in Christian faith is neither as direct nor as clear as some educators suggest. While a develomental theory may emphasize growth as a function of the individual's interaction with the world, it often has tended to focus more on the physical and mental potential of the individual and has not sufficiently described the differences in growth processes in various cultural worlds. For example, even in American culture, significant differences have been discovered between the development of men and that of women. The particularities represented in the faiths, myths, and rituals of different cultural worlds may affect the process of development.

In addition, the reliance on developmental theory in Christian education has tended to coincide with the privatizing of religious experience in America. Religious faith, as well as growth in faith, has come to be seen as a very idiosyncratic process. Correspondingly, Christian education has tended to focus more on the individual than on the community of faith. Questions of one's accountability to others in the faith community and to the world itself have received less and less attention.

Educators must study the meaning of development in the

Christian community. Theological reflection on the relationship between transformation (conversion) and development (nurture) is necessary, as well as direct observation of the interaction of the Christian person with the Christian community. A primary question concerns the power of Christian rituals, social roles, symbols, and stories to effect a deeper understanding and experiencing of God's grace and vision for living. A new kind of developmental research is called for—one that examines the process of Christian faith development. Thought should be given to how this faith is experienced, what its processes of growth may be, and what shape the community of faith must assume in order to facilitate maturity in Christian faith. It will thus deal with both the Christian person and the Christian community, for their relationship is reciprocal. The Christian person is accountable to the community, seeking to know its ways and helping it to more adequately embody and reflect its originating event, the Christ of God; and the community is the context within which faith is experienced and vocation defined.

4. *Christian educators must seek to clarify the relationship of Christian education to the wider learning environment.*

The church may be the primary arena where persons can learn the Christian faith, but it is not the only one. One task for Christian educators is the clarification of arenas where Christian learning takes place; they must coordinate, or at least respond to, these arenas. Again, the situation of pluralism increases the difficulty of such a coordination.

In the heyday of the Sunday school, during the last part of the nineteenth century, Christian education was effected through a wide variety of agencies where values and purposes were consistent. Public school, Sunday school, religious press, church agencies for reform, and church life worked together in a pattern to propagate and support evangelical Protestant faith. The vision of such a coordinated program continued even into the progressive period when religious education leaders argued for the church school, which was defined as a coordinating agency, combining adult instruction, church life, youth societies, mission efforts, and church instruction in a unified program.

In the increased pluralism and secularity of American society, for most mainline denominations the task of Christian education has been increasingly returned to the church itself. (The earlier ecology of Christian education institutions is still maintained for many evangelical churches, some of which coordinate church life, Sunday schools, Christian day schools, television networks, and church press in a unified educational environment.) The church is increasingly forced to provide Christian education without the cultural support upon which it has traditionally relied. Nevertheless, persons continue to learn attitudes, either negative or positive, about Christian faith and values—from the media, whether it be the electronic church, movies, or the secular press; from the public school, in its studies of religions and values and through its "hidden curriculum"; and from society at large, in cultural events, political campaigns, and efforts at human betterment. Each person is in a network of institutions and agencies which formally or informally teach about Christian faith. The media, the place of work, the social context, and the family, together with the efforts of the church, support one another, or conflict, to form a Christian education environment.

Christian education must try to understand the network of institutions and discover approaches to respond to that network. One clear response is the creation of a Christian subculture to insulate its members from the wider plural environment. However, this alternative will not be adequate for most mainline churches that seek to encounter the world, learn from its wisdom, and transform it. It may be necessary to attempt to respond to some of these other educators with our own Christian media, schools, and so on; or at least to become more aware of the effect of these agencies and their patterns of functioning, so that a more comprehensive progam of education can be created.

Throughout history, each religion either has had cultural

support or has found it necessary to create an insulated ghetto in order to flourish. The present situation of religious and cultural pluralism is unique. The Christian church will need to make a significant effort to discover an educational ministry for such a context.

5. *The foundational relationship of Christian education to both educational theory and theology must be explored continually.*

At times, Christian education has drawn from both educational theory and theology in defining its theory and practice and has been weighted toward one direction or the other. For example, in the 1930s, when character study was a predominant concern of religious educators, education was emphasized; in the later 1940s, with the neo-orthodox critique of Christian education, theology was emphasized. In each approach, the relationship must be explored. Fundamentally, this exploration deals with the broader issue of the relationship between theology and the human sciences, or expressed another way, between theological and cultural knowledge.

Christian education is a theological concern, in that at its root are questions about the nature of the Christian community, the processes by which this community transmits and recreates its heritage and the truth and adequacy of the theological conceptions, church rituals, and community symbols through which the content of the faith is expressed. Only by theological analysis can these fundamental questions be addressed. In addition, the question as to which educational resources drawn from the culture may be used to "teach" Christian faith can be answered only on theological grounds.

On the other hand, Christian education is an educational concern, in that it asks basic questions: How does a culture transmit itself? How does it transform its values to respond to new social conditions? The anthropology and sociology of education, teaching and learning theories, and curriculum theories—all contribute to reflection on Christian education. The basic content to be taught, the context within which it is taught, the institutions and vehicles that teach it, the truth of the content, and its power to center an individual and to inform that individual's action in the world—these are also Christian education concerns.

Christian education is therefore foundationally informed by both theology and educational theory; both inform each other and transform each other. For example, developmental theories drawn from education have helped Christian educators sequence Christian content to be understood; and Christian education helped birth a public-school movement which was to be concerned with the care of all persons and the humanization of life.

Despite the reciprocal relationship, we argue for the primacy of theology, as do the other articles in this book. The Christian community is a particular community with particular values, symbols, stories, rituals, and theological formulations which have grown to express the experience of the event of Christ. The content, context, perspective, and structures of Christian education are uniquely related to the experience of that event. It constitutes the Christian community and provides the vehicles by which the community transmits, clarifies, recreates, and embodies its faith in life. Fundamentally, Christian education is a theological praxis by which the community seeks to tell the truth of its story so that it may be heard, believed, and followed. As a theological praxis, Christian education will necessarily be forced to address the question of the relationship of Christ to culture, or the relationship of secular to theological knowledge. Theology therefore sets the terms by which the church uses education and learns from its analysis. To be faithful to the event of Christ, and to tell about it in intelligible ways in new situations, will require Christian educators continually to assess the relationship of theology and education to discover how education can inform theological praxis.

While other issues for the future of Christian education could certainly be stated, this list represents some of the most significant. They all arise out of the disintegration of earlier strategies for Christian education which effectively responded to particular cultural concerns. Christian education continually faces the question of the context within which the church must exist and the meaning of the faith within that context. This continuing struggle is evidence of its attempt to remain faithful to the experience of the revelation of Christ in history.

Shaping the Church's Educational Future

Our survey of dominant metaphors in the field of Christian education is not intended to be exhaustive; other writers may not conform precisely to the concepts presented here. James Michael Lee, for example, proposes an instructional model which stresses the findings of the social sciences. Some would put more emphasis on one-time conversion than did Donald Miller in his model of spiritual development. The faith community model varies according to the church tradition one represents. There are surely other powerful living metaphors not included among these five, but any account of the future of Christian education must take into account those we have presented.

In order for Christian education to remain a powerful expression of Christian mission in the future, attention must be given to three levels: the local church, denominational staff, and academic study.

Christian education at the local church level has been much criticized in the past several decades. Whether because of social analysis of the Sunday school as the legitimation of self-centered cultural values, or earlier pronouncements that the school model is dead, many have been heavily critical of the congregation's effort to educate. But congregational education has continued, new curricula have been developed, and new programs have been originated in spite of the competition of television, the explosion of leisure-time opportunities, and the changing role of women and families in society.

The future of Christian education must affirm the congregations in their efforts. Suggestions about styles of teaching, educational planning, and new modes of learning may be taken more seriously when local congregations perceive that they support and strengthen their programs, rather than destroy them. It is time for words of affirmation. All things considered, local churches have done a remarkable job in nurturing faith, and their continuing dedication needs to be celebrated as the context for any suggested innovation.

At the denominational level, Christian education must allow for multiple possibilities. The variety of educational images now shaping the field surely indicate that no one way will be sufficient in the future. Denominational and interdenominational educators should work together to explore the various options. It would be best to relate to local congregations in a variety of ways. Imaginative new methods for providing curriculum are needed. The models discussed in this book offer suggestions for new procedures at the denominational level.

At the academic level, Christian education should be studied from two aspects. One viewpoint presents the various assumptions of theology; the other, the foundational elements of education and the related disciplines of psychology, sociology, and management. Current practice and new trends must be examined critically from both aspects if education is to make a significant contribution to the future. In addition, it is crucial that the academic world continue the analysis of emerging metaphors.

The gospel itself will be impoverished if the educational efforts of Christians are impoverished. A vital future for the church's educational program will require local, denominational, interdenominational, and academic cooperation. We hope these essays are a contribution in that direction.

Notes

Chapter 1. Approaches

1. Allen J. Moore, ed., *Report of the Task Force on Defining the Academic Discipline of Religious Education*, 2 vols. (Nashville: The Board of Discipleship of The United Methodist Church, 1980).

2. Iris Cully, "What Killed Religious Education," *Religion in Life* 40 (Autumn 1971): 404-11.

3. See Ian Barbour, *Myths, Models and Paradigms* (New York: Harper & Row, 1974); Peter Berger and Thomas Luckmann, *The Social Construction of Reality* (New York: Doubleday & Co., 1966).

4. See David Tracy, *Blessed Rage for Order* (New York: Seabury Press, 1975); James Macdonald, "A Transcendental Developmental Ideology of Education," *Heightened Consciousness, Cultural Revolution, and Curriculum Theory*, ed. William Pinar (Berkeley, Cal.: McCutchan Publishing Corp., 1974). For Christian education, see Gloria Durka and Joanmarie Smith, eds., *Emerging Issues in Religious Education* (New York: Paulist Press, 1976); Berard L. Marthaler, "Toward a Revisionist Model in Catechetics (Reflections on David Tracy's *Blessed Rage for Order*)," *The Living Light* 13 (Fall 1976): 458-69.

5. Tracy, *Blessed Rage for Order*, p. 32. Chs. 2 and 3 include the analysis of theological options and the proposed revisionist position.

6. Macdonald, "Transcendental Developmental Ideology," pp. 104-5.

7. Parenthetically, each of these approaches represents a distinctive theology of the church. They parallel the typology presented by Avery Dulles, *Models of the Church* (Garden City, N.J.: Doubleday & Co., 1974).

8. Both contemporary and historical Christian education theorists will be used to illustrate each of these approaches to Christian education. Since the typology is meant to be descriptive, in no case can the work of a particular theorist be contained by the simple description of each type. The thought of each theorist is more complex, and the works of some overlap the types. Nevertheless, each shows how foundational themes and metaphors can be developed to provide a Christian education theory and practice.

9. James Michael Lee, *The Flow of Religious Instruction: A Social Science Approach* (Mishawaka, Ind.: Religious Education Press, 1973), p. 269.

10. J.M. Gregory, "The Future of the Sunday School," *The Sunday School Teacher* 2 (June 1867): 173.

11. James Michael Lee, *The Shape of Religious Instruction: A Social Science Approach* (Mishawaka, Ind.: Religious Education Press, 1971), p. 74.

12. Lee, *Flow of Religious Instruction*, pp. 48-49.

13. Lee, *Shape of Religious Instruction*, pp. 81-88.

14. *Ibid.*, p. 51.

15. Edward Eggleston, "The Uniform Lesson Question," *The Fifth National Sunday-School Convention* (New York: Aug. O. Van Lennep, 1872), p. 92.

16. John Westerhoff, III, *Will Our Children Have Faith?* (New York: Seabury Press, 1976), p. 9.

17. John Westerhoff, III, "A Call to Catechesis (A Response to Charles Melchert)," *The Living Light* 14 (Fall 1977): 358.

18. Westerhoff, "Call to Catechesis," pp. 356-57.

19. *Ibid.*, p. 357.

20. Westerhoff, *Will Our Children Have Faith?*, pp. 38-42, 49-50.

21. Urban T. Holmes, III, and John H. Westerhoff, III, *Christian Believing* (New York: Seabury Press, 1979), pp. 83, 87.

22. The International Council of Religious Education, *The Development of a Curriculum of Religious Education* (Chicago: International Council of Religious Education, 1928), pp. 14-15.

23. Gloria Durka and Joanmarie Smith, "Modeling in Religious Education," *Religious Education* 71 (March/April 1976): 127-32.

24. See James W. Fowler, *Stages of Faith* (New York: Harper & Row, 1981); Donald Miller, *The Wing-Footed Wanderer* (Nashville: Abingdon, 1977); James Whitehead and Evelyn Whitehead, *Christian Life Patterns* (Garden City, N.J.: Doubleday &

Co., 1979); Mary Wilcox, *Developmental Journey* (Nashville: Abingdon, 1978).

25. Ross Snyder, *On Becoming Human: Discovering Yourself and Your Life World* (Nashville: Abingdon Press, 1967).

26. See *Centerquest: Teacher's Manual, Adult Classes* (St. Louis, Mo.: Educational Center, 1979), pp. 5-29.

27. Henry Ward Beecher, "The Mission Work of the Sunday School," *The Third National Sunday School Convention* (Philadelphia: J.C. Garrigues & Co., 1869), pp. 73, 77.

28. Malcolm Warford, *The Necessary Illusion: Church Culture and Educational Change* (Philadelphia: Pilgrim Press, 1976), p. 54.

29. See Grant Shockley, "Liberation Theology, Black Theology and Religious Education," *Foundation for Christian Education in an Era of Change*, ed. Marvin Taylor (Nashville: Abingdon, 1976); Brian Wren, *Education for Justice: Pedagogical Principles* (Maryknoll, N.Y.: Orbis Books, 1977).

30. William Clayton Bower, "Christian Education After Nineteen Centuries," *Religion in Life* 7 (Winter 1942-43): 46.

31. Thomas Groome, *Christian Religious Education: Sharing Our Story and Vision* (New York: Harper & Row, 1980), p. 195.

32. Douglas Wingeier, *Working Out Your Own Beliefs: A Guide for Doing Your Own Theology* (Nashville: Abingdon, 1980), p. 7.

33. *Ibid.*, pp. 197-98.

Chapter 2. Religious Instruction

1. Lee to Jack Seymour, April 16, 1980.

2. Thomas Green, *The Activities of Teaching* (New York: McGraw-Hill, 1971), p. 29.

3. *Ibid.*, p. 103.

4. Harry S. Broudy, "Types of Knowledge and Purposes of Education," *Schooling and the Acquisition of Knowledge*, ed. Richard C. Anderson, Rand J. Spiro, and Williams E. Montague (Hillsdale, N.J.: Lawrence Erlbaum Associates, 1977), pp. 12-15.

5. Paul Tillich, *Theology of Culture* (New York: Oxford University Press, 1959), p. 201.

6. Thomas Aquinas, "The Teacher," *Basic Writings in Christian Education*, ed. Kendig Brubaker Cully (Philadelphia: Westminster Press, 1960), pp. 108-9.

7. Marc Belth, *The Process of Thinking* (New York: David McKay, 1977), p. xii.

8. Charles Melchert, "Understanding and Religious Education," *Process and Relationship*, ed. Iris V. Cully and Kendig Brubaker Cully (Birmingham, Ala.: Religious Education Press, 1978), pp. 41-48.

9. Stephen Toulmin, *Human Understanding*, Vol. I, *The Collective Use and Evolution of Concepts* (Princeton, N.J.: Princeton University Press, 1972), p. 35.

10. Report of Harvard Committee, *General Education in a Free Society* (Cambridge: Harvard University Press, 1945), p. 105.

11. *Religion in America 1979–80* (Princeton, N.J.: Princeton Religious Research Center, 1980), p. 1.

12. Hanna Arendt, *The Life of the Mind*, Vol. I, *Thinking* (New York: Harcourt Brace Jovanovich, 1971), pp. 3-5.

13. Belth, *Process of Thinking*, p. xxi.

14. Green, *Activities of Teaching*, p. 53.

15. Quoted by Martin Marty, *A Nation of Behavers* (Chicago: University of Chicago Press, 1976), p. 46.

16. Green, *Activities of Teaching*, p. 53.

17. This matter is developed quite fully in James Borhek and Richard Curtis, *A Sociology of Belief* (New York: John Wiley & Sons, 1975).

18. See David G. Myers, *The Human Puzzle: Psychological Research and Christian Belief* (San Francisco: Harper & Row, 1978).

19. Locke Bowman, *Teaching Today: The Church's First Ministry* (Philadelphia: Westminster Press, 1980), p. 150.

20. See Sara Little, "Ways of Knowing: An Approach to Teaching about Teaching," *Process and Relationship*, ed. Cully and Cully, pp. 15-21.

21. Quoted by Edward B. Lindaman, "Thinking in the Future Tense," *The Church and the '80's: Theology, News, and Notes*, Fuller Theological Seminary (June 1979): 5.

Chapter 3. Faith Community

1. Alex Haley, *Roots* (New York: Doubleday & Co., 1976).

2. Robert A. Evans, "The Quest for Community," *Union Seminary Quarterly Review* 30 (Winter-Summer 1975): 197.

3. C. Ellis Nelson, *Where Faith Begins* (Richmond: John Knox Press, 1967). Also John H. Westerhoff III, *Will Our Children Have Faith?* (New York: Seabury Press, 1976) and *Inner Growth, Outer Change: An Educational Guide to Church Renewal* (New York: Seabury Press, 1979); with Gwen Kennedy Neville,

Generation to Generation: Conversations on Religious Education and Culture (Philadelphia: Pilgrim Press, 1974) and *Learning through Liturgy* (New York: Seabury Press, 1978).

4. I am not disagreeing, at this point, with Westerhoff's critique of the effectiveness of the Sunday school in the nurture of faith, or with his disillusionment with the Protestant preoccupation with the Sunday school as the agency of its educational ministry. But my agreement with him at these points notwithstanding, I believe that a "school" in some form is still important in the transmission of values, beliefs, and practices from one generation to the next.

Chapter 4. Development

1. Horace Bushnell, *Christian Nurture* (Grand Rapids, Mich.: Baker Book House, 1979).
2. Plato, selections from *The Republic,* in Robert Ulich, *Three Thousand Years of Educational Wisdom,* 2nd ed. (Cambridge, Mass.: Harvard University Press, 1954), pp. 31-61.
3. Jean Jacques Rousseau, selections from *Emile,* in Ulich, *Educational Wisdom,* p. 423.
4. R.S. Peters, "Education and Human Development," *Education and Reason,* ed. R.F. Dearden, P.H. Hirst, and R.S. Peters (London: Routledge & Kegan Paul, 1975), p. 112.
5. *Ibid.*
6. A good single source of the many works of Jean Piaget is Piaget and Barbara Inhelder, *The Psychology of the Child* (New York: Basic Books, 1969).
7. Ronald Goldman, *Readiness for Religion* (London: Routledge & Kegan Paul, 1965).
8. *Ibid.,* p. 80.
9. Lawrence Kohlberg, "From Is to Ought: How to Commit the Naturalistic Fallacy and Get Away with It in the Study of Moral Development," *Cognitive Development and Epistemology,* ed. Theodore Mischel (New York: Academic Press, 1971).
10. Craig Dykstra, "Moral Virtue or Social Reasoning," *Religious Education* 75 (March-April 1980): 115-28; Carol Gilligan, "In a Different Voice: Women's Conception of the Self and of Morality," *Harvard Educational Review* 47 (November 1977): 481-517; Ralph B. Potter, "Justice and Beyond in Moral Education" (Address delivered at the Regional Conference on

the Moral Development of Youth, Wayzata, Minn., June 1, 1977).

11. Erik Erikson, *Identity and the Life Cycle, Psychological Issues,* Vol. 1 (New York: International Universities Press, 1959), pp. 40-100.

12. *Ibid.,* p. 56.

13. Mary M. Wilcox, *Developmental Journey* (Nashville: Abingdon, 1979), p. 194.

14. Peters, "Education and Human Development," pp. 125-26.

15. Donald Evans, *Struggle and Fulfillment* (New York: Collins Publishing Co., 1979).

16. Donald E. Miller, *The Wing-Footed Wanderer* (Nashville: Abingdon, 1977), pp. 123-29.

17. James Fowler, *Stages of Faith* (New York: Harper & Row, 1981).

18. Thomas C. Hennesey, S.J., ed., *Values and Moral Development* (New York: Paulist Press, 1976), p. 184.

19. H. Richard Niebuhr, *The Responsible Self* (New York: Harper & Row, 1963).

Chapter 5. Liberation

1. The popularity of books in this area is well known although the general public does not seem to grasp the urgency of the situation. See, e.g., Alvin Toffler, *The Third Wave* (New York: Wm. Morrow & Co., 1980), and *Future Shock* (New York: Random House, 1970).

2. Both the "globalization" of education and the *inter*dependency of *all* life have received much attention recently and have been a major concern of the faculty at the School of Theology at Claremont. Also see publications of the Department of Development Education, World Council of Churches.

3. Paulo Freire, "Education, Liberation, and the Church," *Study Encounter* 9/1 (1973). Also see Malcolm L. Warford, *The Necessary Illusion* (Philadelphia: Pilgrim Press, 1976), pp. 68-69.

4. An example of the way affluent Americans imitate the way of the poor can be found in the "hippie" movement of the 1960s. See, e.g., Allen J. Moore, "The Revolt against Affluence," *Religion in Life* 37 (Winter 1968): 509-18. The environmentalists of the 1970s also express the preoccupation of materialistic people with poverty and the life-style of simpler living. The subjective aspect of this quest for experience in itself denies the political praxis called for in liberation education.

5. Juan Luis Segundo, *The Liberation of Theology* (Maryknoll, N.Y.: Orbis Books, 1976), pp. 3-4. Also see Segundo, *The Hidden Motives of Pastoral Action* (Maryknoll, N.Y.: Orbis Books, 1978).

6. Segundo, *Liberation of Theology,* pp. 8-9.

7. An example is the readiness with which we have appropriated the liberationist idea that salvation is liberation. We fail to grasp that in the Latin American scene, liberation refers to *political* liberation.

8. Christian education in North America takes place in a world context in which 20% of the people control 80% of the world's resources, and two-thirds of the human family are in various states of starvation and hunger. We have conditioned ourselves to be immune to the fact that whites are the haves and that nonwhites are the poor. Much mainline theology has served to justify this gross discrimination by overtones of "blessed" and the idea of stewardship.

9. Don Browning, *The Moral Context of Pastoral Care* (Philadelphia: Westminster Press, 1976).

10. This discussion is adapted from Allen J. Moore, "Life Style Education" (Lecture given at the Consultation for Local Church Leaders on Hunger and Life Style Changes, Scarritt College, Nashville, Tenn., October 30-November 1, 1979). Also see Moore, "The Problems of Life Style," *Christian Advocate* (January 7, 1971) and "Sexual Life Style," *Engage* (December 1972).

11. Paulo Freire, "Conscientizing as a Way of Liberating," *Paulo Freire,* ed. LADOC (Washington, D.C.: Division of Latin America, U.S.C.C., n.d.), pp. 3-4.

12. *Ibid.,* p. 5.

13. Segundo, *Hidden Motives of Pastoral Action.*

14. In addition to the seminal writings of Segundo, there are a variety of other liberationists who confront the church with its oppressive way, e.g., Jürgen Moltmann, Mary Daly, James Cone, Penelope Washbourn, Johannes B. Metz, Gustavo Gutiérrez, and Rubem Alves.

15. Penelope Washbourn, "Authority of Idolatry? Feminine Theology and the Church," *The Christian Century* 92 (October 29, 1975): 964.

16. Robert McAfee Brown, *Is Our Faith Obsolete?* (Philadelphia: Westminster Press, 1974), p. 129.

17. For a similar and more exhaustive critique of religious education, see Donald E. Miller, "Religious Education and

Social Change," manuscript (Bethany Seminary, Chicago, 1969).

18. Segundo, *Liberation of Theology*, p. 9.

19. A further development of this point can be found in Allen J. Moore, "Toward a Theology of Christian Education for the 1980's," photocopy (School of Theology at Claremont, Claremont, Cal., 1978).

20. See William Pinar, ed., *Curriculum Theorizing: The Reconceptualists* (Berkeley, Cal.: McCutchan Publishing Corp., 1974).

21.. Ivan Illich, "Education: A Consumer Commodity and a Pseudo-Religion," *The Christian Century* 88 (December 15, 1971): 1464-65.

22. Dwayne Huebner, "Curriculum as Concern for Man's Temporality," *Curriculum Theorizing*, ed. Pinar, pp. 237-49.

23. A phrase used by James Fowler. Also see the work of Thomas H. Groome, e.g., *Christian Religious Education: Sharing Our Story and Vision* (San Francisco: Harper & Row, 1980).

Chapter 6. Interpretation

1. See Richard E. Palmer, *Hermeneutics* (Evanston, Ill.: Northwestern University Press, 1969), pp. 8-10.

2. See Paul Ricoeur, *Interpretation Theory: Discourse and the Surplus of Meaning* (Fort Worth: Texas Christian University Press, 1976).

3. Raimundo Panikkar, *Myth, Faith and Hermeneutics* (New York: Paulist Press, 1979), p. 8.

4. Paul Ricoeur, "The Model of the Text: Meaningful Action Considered as Text," *Social Research* 38 (Autumn 1971): 529-62.

5. See James MacDonald, "A Transcendental Developmental Ideology of Education," *Heightened Consciousness, Cultural Revolution and Curriculum Theory*, ed. William Pinar (Berkeley, Cal.: McCutchan Publishing Corp., 1974), pp. 94-97.

6. Panikkar, *Myth, Faith and Hermeneutics*, pp. 8-9.

7. *Ibid.*, p. 9.

8. *Ibid.*, pp. 453-55.

9. For one example of this approach using a particular theology—i.e., a theology of hope—see Jack Seymour, "Education for the Kingdom: Leadership in Tomorrow's Church," *Chicago Theological Seminary Register* 69 (Fall 1979): 11-21.

10. Wilfred Cantwell Smith, *Faith and Belief* (Princeton, N.J.: Princeton University Press, 1979), pp. 103-27.
11. Charles Winquist, *Practical Hermeneutics: A Revised Agenda For Ministry* (Chico, Cal.: Scholars Press, 1980), pp. 91-93.
12. *Ibid.*, p. 59.
13. Thomas Groome, *Christian Religious Education: Sharing Our Story and Vision* (San Francisco: Harper & Row, 1980), pp. 261-74.
14. Hubert Halbfas, *Theory of Catechetics: Language and Experience in Religious Education* (New York: Herder & Herder, 1971), p. 149.
15. See Winquist, *Practical Hermeneutics*, pp. 18, 40, 41.
16. See Victor Turner, *Dramas, Fields and Metaphors: Symbolic Action in Human Society* (Ithaca, N.Y.: Cornell University Press, 1974); Victor Turner and Edith Turner, *Image and Pilgrimage in Christian Culture: Anthropological Perspectives* (New York: Columbia University Press, 1978). This description of pilgrimage in Christian culture is drawn from these sources.
17. Turner, *Image and Pilgrimage*, pp. 7-8.
18. *Ibid.*, p. 11.
19. E.g., in exegesis, see how Walter Wink uses psychology; Robin Scroggs, sociology; and Daniel Patte and Aline Patte, structural analysis: Wink, *The Bible in Human Transformation* (Philadelphia: Fortress Press, 1973); Scroggs, "The Sociological Interpretation of the New Testament: The Present State of Research," *New Testament Studies* 26 (January 1980): 164-79; Patte and Patte, *Structural Exegesis: From Theory to Practice* (Philadelphia: Fortress Press, 1978).
20. For these insights, we are indebted to the work of Groome, *Christian Religious Education;* James Whitehead and Evelyn Whitehead, *Method in Ministry* (New York: Seabury Press, 1980); Winquist, *Practical Hermeneutics*.
21. Panikkar, *Myth, Faith and Hermeneutics*, p. 10.

Contributors

Charles R. Foster—professor of Christian education, Scarritt College, Nashville, Tennessee

Sara P. Little—Robert and Lucy Reynolds Critz Professor of Christian Education, Union Theological Seminary in Virginia, Richmond, Virginia

Donald E. Miller—professor of Christian education and ethics and director of graduate studies, Bethany Theological Seminary, Oak Brook, Illinois

Allen J. Moore—professor of religion and personality and Christian education, School of Theology at Claremont, Claremont, California

Jack L. Seymour—assistant professor of Christian education, Scarritt College, Nashville, Tennessee

Carol A. Wehrheim—assistant director of the Doctor of Ministry Program, McCormick Theological Seminary, Chicago, Illinois